The Personal Tutor

Palgrave Study Guides

Authoring a PhD
Critical Thinking Skills
Career Skills
e-Learning Skills
Effective Communication for
    Arts and Humanities Students
Effective Communication for
    Science and Technology
The Exam Skills Handbook
The Foundations of Research
The Good Supervisor
How to Manage your Arts, Humanities and
    Social Science Degree
How to Manage your Distance and
    Open Learning Course
How to Manage your Postgraduate Course
How to Manage your Science and
    Technology Degree
How to Study Foreign Languages
How to Write Better Essays
IT Skills for Successful Study
Making Sense of Statistics
The Mature Student's Guide to Writing (2nd edn)
The Palgrave Student Planner
The Personal Tutor's Handbook
The Postgraduate Research Handbook
Presentation Skills for Students

The Principles of Writing in Psychology
Professional Writing (2nd edn)
Research Using IT
Skills for Success
The Student Life Handbook
The Student's Guide to Writing (2nd edn)
The Study Abroad Handbook
The Study Skills Handbook (2nd edn)
Study Skills for Speakers of English as
    a Second Language
Studying Buiness at MBA and Masters Level
Studying the Built Environment
Studying Economics
Studying History (3rd edn)
Studying Law
Studying Mathematics and its Applications
Studying Modern Drama (2nd edn)
Studying Physics
Studying Programming
Studying Psychology (2nd edn)
Teaching Study Skills and Supporting Learning
Work Placements – a Survival Guide for Students
Write it Right
Writing for Engineers (3rd edn)

Palgrave Study Guides: Literature
General Editors: John Peck and Martin Coyle

How to Begin Studying English Literature
    (3rd edn)
How to Study a Jane Austen Novel (2nd edn)
How to Study a Charles Dickens Novel
How to Study Chaucer (2nd edn)
How to Study an E. M. Forster Novel
How to Study James Joyce
How to Study Linguistics (2nd edn)

How to Study Modern Poetry
How to Study a Novel (2nd edn)
How to Study a Poet
How to Study a Renaissance Play
How to Study Romantic Poetry (2nd edn)
How to Study a Shakespeare Play (2nd edn)
How to Study Television
Practical Criticism

The Personal Tutor's Handbook

Lindsey Neville

First published 2007 by
PALGRAVE MACMILLAN
Houndmills, Basingstoke, Hampshire RG21 6XS and
175 Fifth Avenue, New York, N.Y. 10010
Companies and representatives throughout the world

PALGRAVE MACMILLAN is the global academic imprint of the Palgrave
Macmillan division of St. Martin's Press, LLC and of Palgrave Macmillan Ltd.
Macmillan® is a registered trademark in the United States, United Kingdom
and other countries. Palgrave is a registered trademark in the European
Union and other countries.

ISBN-13: 978–0–230–50789–0
ISBN-10: 0–230–50789–1

This book is printed on paper suitable for recycling and made from fully
managed and sustained forest sources. Logging, pulping and manufacturing
processes are expected to conform to the environmental regulations of the
country of origin.

A catalogue record for this book is available from the British Library.

10   9   8   7   6   5   4   3   2   1
16   15   14   13   12   11   10   09   08   07

Printed and bound in Great Britain by
Creative Print & Design (Wales), Ebbw Vale

Contents

Acknowledgements

There are a number of people without whom this book would not have reached publication:

- students and staff of the University of Worcester for offering their experiences of personal tutoring for the initial research;
- my family and friends for their encouragement and forbearance;
- the contributors for their enthusiasm for the project and willingness to work to my deadlines;
- Suzannah Burywood and Karen Griffiths at Palgrave Macmillan for their patience and enthusiasm for the project.

Thank you to you all.

L.N.

Foreword

Higher education has changed dramatically since 1992 when Jan Birtle and I wrote a book called *Handbook for Personal Tutors in Higher Education*, and it is surprising that no other book has been written on this crucial topic until now. The expansion of student numbers in higher education has not been matched by increased resources, resulting in less face-to-face contact between students and academic staff. At the same time, students – particularly those recruited to fulfil the widening participation agenda and to enhance equal opportunities – need even more help, support and guidance with their academic work and personal concerns. The economic imperative that drives expansion fuels a consumer culture, with students driven towards achievement that promises employment and a career rather than providing them with opportunities for academic exploration, personal growth and development. Modularisation provides bite-sized rewards for individuals but mitigates against cohesion, belonging and support from a familiar cohort of staff and students. At the same time the massification of higher education requires increased bureaucracy. The sheer cost invites increased government monitoring to ensure value for money; the Research Assessment exercise drives a significant proportion of the funding resource; and these factors result in an increased administrative burden and pressure on academic staff to engage in research. Meanwhile students have their own problems, fees, living costs and the need to work part time to fund themselves. Students have never needed more support and had access to less. Personal tutoring can provide the vital link that cuts across the bureaucracy and makes the higher education experience more human. Personal tutors will be rewarded by the relationships they forge with students, but recognition by their institutions for these efforts is often in short supply.

Higher education poses many challenges for its staff. A system of mass higher education maintains many qualities of an elite system including an interface between teaching and research and a tradition of 'academic intimacy' characterised by pastoral care and a commitment to students' support systems. At the same time autonomy has been eroded and the state's increasing imposition of quality assurance systems for administration, teaching and research that drive funding formulae cannot be ignored.

While the Labour Party's aim to see 50 per cent of young people benefiting from higher education is laudable, its aim is not just to provide a comprehensive educational experience for the individual, but also to ensure a skilled and educated workforce to promote the economic development of Britain in the future. The expansion of places in higher education was very fast, with hastily conceived building programmes and expansion in student numbers without a corresponding expansion in staff and resources. At the same time, universities have become more complex institutions, inviting managerialism, with their administration centrally managed and controlled in ways that work against the more traditional collegial systems, in which cooperation and communication were fundamental principles. Such institutions command more public expenditure, which in turn prompts governmental control – monitoring, setting objectives and making comparisons through league tables. The good news for the provision of personal tutorial systems is that the student experience also features in tables, providing an important impetus for them to be nurtured.

These same league tables also feature completion rates; a major concern for some institutions particularly where widening participation has been a feature of recruitment. Reasons for non-completion of higher education courses varies between students, but important factors that govern withdrawal include poor quality of student experience, inability to cope with the demands of the programme, unhappiness with the social environment, a wrong choice of programme, matters relating to financial need and dissatisfaction with aspects of institutional provision.

Students are away from home, under stress and experiencing new pressures. They are often young adults just maturing: it is a time of vulnerability. Many universities have complex and sophisticated central support services, including mental health workers as well as counsellors, careers officers, disability and welfare provision and study support tutors. While such services are highly valued and welcome, they also suffer from centralised control and bureaucratisation. Students and their tutors shop for a service, prompting a swift referral to the relevant provider to meet the identified need. Such services are valuable and can function well as long as students' needs are recognised. Some students will propel themselves to seek assistance but many need support and guidance, and encouragement.

This is the backdrop against which the activity of personal tutoring takes place. Personal tutors are these same academics who are overworked and underpaid, expected to achieve excellence in teaching administration and research (or else no performance-related pay), who teach and examine large classes in a stressful environment, as well as encouraging their students to be reflective and self-evaluative. They are expected to help students survive and achieve. A well-functioning personal tutorial system that comprehensively embraces the whole student body provides a web of support that captures all the potential problems for which solutions can be sought. Every student, old or young needs to connect with the university system through a personal tutor and in some instances with their tutorial group. They need to build a relationship with their tutor and to build the confidence that enables them to reveal their difficulties when times are hard.

This book provides just what personal tutors need to help them negotiate and manage the complexities of serving the needs of the students and the organisation. It will enable them to consider the impact on both staff and students of the changing face of higher education and gain insight and understanding into the diverse needs of a multicultural student body. There are recommendations for practice at the end of each chapter that will encourage tutors to reflect on their experience and add new skills to their repertoire. Personal tutors are essential to successful and humane higher education institutions. This book is essential reading for those who want to make a difference in the academic and personal lives of their tutees and to make a valuable contribution to the overall success of their institution.

Sue Wheeler
Institute of Lifelong Learning
University of Leicester

Notes on the Contributors

Alexa Collicott has experience as a part-time lecturer at the University of Gloucestershire. She has worked in arts marketing at the Almeida Theatre, London and the Roses' Theatre, Tewkesbury. She is currently involved in an Arts Council funded community arts project at the Everyman Theatre, Cheltenham.

Annie Grant is the Dean of Students and Director of Student Services at the University of East Anglia. Following an academic career, she moved to the University of Leicester in 1991, first directing a learning and teaching initiative and then establishing and directing the Educational Development and Support Centre. She took up her current post at UEA in 2004. She has undertaken a number of consultancies for UK and international higher education institutions (HEIs) on areas that include student skills development, provision for students with disabilities and mental health difficulties, and learning and teaching. She has also published on these topics and on archaeology, her academic discipline. She has a strong commitment to widening participation and promoting equality of opportunity and has a particular interest in the interface between the academic and student guidance and support functions of HEIs.

Rebecca Harrison is Deputy Head of Student Services at the University College for Creative Arts. She has worked in higher education for fifteen years at universities in the United States, Egypt and England. With a strong interest in diversity she has led projects at several universities to improve support for students with disabilities, international students and ethnic minority students from families with no tradition of higher education. In 2002 she served on a joint UKCOSA (the Council for International Education) and Skill working group to explore the issue of support for international students with disabilities.

Elizabeth Hewitt is a British Association for Counselling and Psychotherapy (BACP) Accredited Counsellor and is Senior Counsellor at the University of

Worcester. She has worked as a counsellor and supervisor in various organ-isational settings and in private practice. She is also an experienced family mediator. Before becoming a counsellor she taught in both secondary and higher education, and she has continued to work as a trainer and tutor on counselling programmes in the tertiary sector in recent years. Her long-standing experience of the role of the tutor is now part of her wider interest in the interface between those who support students and the institution of which they are a part.

Lindsey Neville is currently a Senior Lecturer in Community and Social Welfare in the Institute of Health, Social Care and Psychology at the University of Worcester. She has qualified teacher status and has taught in primary, secondary, and further education settings. As the counsellor at a college of further education she developed an interest in the work of the personal tutor. She is an accredited practitioner of both the British Association for Counselling and Psychotherapy and the Higher Education Academy.

Richard Price is a medical doctor who qualified in 1986 and became a partner in general practice in 1992. In 1995 he took up a sessional lecturer's post in the medical school at Newcastle University. Part of that role included responsibility for undergraduate personal tutees. Since 2001 he has been Course Director and tutor for the Graduate Entry to Medicine course at Newcastle. As part of this role he has experience in helping tutees deal with a wide range of personal issues that impinge on their studies.

Sue Wheeler is Professor of Counselling and Psychotherapy at the University of Leicester Institute of Lifelong Learning. As the University counsellor at Aston University between 1985 and 1990 she took a keen interest in the development of the pastoral care system and the training of personal tutors. She is the author (with Jan Birtle) of *A Handbook for Personal Tutors*, published by the Open University Press (1993). She has been invited to be a consultant to several universities who have been revising their personal tuto-rial systems and has offered training to their staff. She now manages a broad programme of counselling and psychotherapy courses, all of which have personal tutoring as an essential aspect of their teaching provision. Her research interests include assessment, mentoring and supervision, the personal qualities of counsellors and psychotherapists, and staff develop-ment.

Part One

Background

1 Introduction

Lindsey Neville

As both a British Association for Counselling and Psychotherapy (BACP) Accredited Counsellor and a Registered Practitioner of the Higher Education Academy (HEA), my interest in my work, as a Senior Lecturer in Community and Social Welfare, spanned the divide between the academic and personal needs of my students. It became evident that progression within the profession was largely only a result of management responsibility or substantial research. In my own institution, I can think of no one who has climbed the career ladder on the strength of their work as a personal tutor. Anecdotal evidence suggests that this is also the case in other institutions. This is usually work that goes on literally and metaphorically behind closed doors and without accolades. Therefore there appears to be an incongruity between the importance of the work to the future of our institutions and our country, and the value that is currently placed on it.

Success in the education profession has been, throughout my career, based on a variety of criteria, none of them apparently directly related to the ability of the students to access the learning offered. Training as a teacher in the 1970s engendered a feeling within those of us instructed in the philosophy, psychology and sociology of education that it was an end in itself, a complete training for a professional life in education. At that time it seemed as if there was a preciousness about the qualification that exempted us from continuing professional development. Despite the esteem with which the profession held its own qualification, I cannot recall any mention being made of developing understanding or skills in the personal issues that affect learners. I cannot remember any sessions during which we discussed students' personal problems or circumstances and the pastoral support that we might be required to provide.

Throughout my teaching career in primary, special, secondary and further education, class management appeared to measure success. The use of a wide variety of learning and teaching methods kept my students reasonably interested, and consequently I was rewarded with a reputation for well-managed classes where I hoped that the students were also actively engaged in learning. However, on reflection I think that this consideration of student learning was far from central to the aims of the schools, or even perhaps my own. It seems that success in the classroom did not take into account the pastoral support that we now need to equate with our teaching and learning role.

The increasing numbers of students entering higher education since 1992 (Higher Education Statistics Agency [HESA], 2005) have created a different kind of academic community from that which my own contemporaries experienced in the 1970s. At that time my own personal tutor had a commitment to six students; colleagues today are more likely to have 24 personal students. We had to meet with her each week to discuss any issues that might affect our personal and professional development. Although counselling was not offered or readily available, students who were seen as vulnerable by personal tutors were drawn to the attention of the on-site Health Centre staff. Despite what seems like a personal and robust approach there were still tragic consequences for students who were struggling with poor mental health, at a time when there was little awareness of the impact of these issues amongst young people. As the Sabbatical President of the Students' Union, I became involved for the first time in the emotional issues affecting young people, when a fellow student and friend committed suicide. Looking back, his death was the beginning of a growing awareness of the importance of talking therapies in helping individuals cope with difficult areas of their lives (Neville, 2004). This book is perhaps another way of highlighting the importance of student support and is dedicated to his memory.

The Postgraduate Certificate in Teaching and Learning in Higher Education was an opportunity to demonstrate competence in both the academic and pastoral support of students and to develop a portfolio which would evidence their interrelatedness. As I did so it quickly became apparent that much of the literature pre-dated the 1992 changes in higher education (HE). It was for this reason that I chose to research the subject of personal tutoring for my MA (Education). Presenting this research at the inaugural Personal Tutoring Conference at the University of Westminster in 2005 demonstrated that there was now an interest in this aspect of the work. This conference resulted in the excellent publication *Personal Tutoring in Higher Education* edited by Liz Thomas and Paula Hixenbaugh. Their book 'fills a gap in the research and development of personal tutoring in the 21st century' (Thomas and Hixenbaugh, 2006). It explores alternative approaches to student support.

The *Personal Tutor's Handbook* takes a different look at the same theme, offering an in-depth insight into staff and student experiences of a university personal tutor system through the use of case studies. It considers the impact on both students and staff of the changing world of higher education and reflects the diversity and equality which must be integral to our practice. There is less focus on the systems and policies that provide the framework for personal tutoring and more on the practical ways in which practitioners can undertake the work to enhance the experience for the benefit of both staff and students. The emphasis is on the day-to-day work of the personal tutor. It does not seek to address entrenched social issues but to provide a starting point for understanding the work. Dryden (1991) highlights Lazarus's counselling principle about knowing your own limitations and others' strengths. This principle seems to be equally valid for the personal tutor and is an underlying focus of the book.

The book aims to explore where the personal tutor's work ends and that of other support services begins. It highlights the key issues in personal tutoring and identifies ways of working within a suggested model of best practice. Much of the text is based on my own research but this is supported by other practitioners. The subject is explored from the differing perspectives of all those involved in personal tutoring in higher education. The emphasis throughout is on recording the experience of those who are engaged in the work, in the hope that it will encourage debate and offer a range of suggestions that others may like to try. In this way it seeks to offer support by practitioner to practitioner.

The subject matter presented in the case studies is representative of the variety of issues raised by students in tutorials. The range presented is not exclusive, but it is hoped that by working through the book the reader will get an understanding of possible approaches to the multiplicity of problems that can be raised by students as part of the tutorial.

The text will assist new academic staff in their role as personal tutor and provide the information and support needed to fulfil the requirements of courses leading to accreditation with the HEA. To successfully complete an appropriate course and achieve accreditation the teachers must show evidence that they have 'provided support to students on academic and pastoral matters in a way which is acceptable to a wide range of students'. The chapters in this book will also evidence the new demands facing existing lecturers in higher education who are adapting to the challenges of post-1992 higher education as they seek to provide effective support to students from diverse backgrounds.

Throughout the text, the tutor is viewed as part of a package of student services which focus on improving retention figures at the same time as enabling students to maximise their educational opportunities (Association of University College Counsellors [AUCC], 1999). It will examine the issues through a number of different perspectives of the role: those of the institution, student and tutor.

Narratives, using the technique of recall, will serve to depict the different 'voices' of both staff and students. They will introduce the reader to the subject and will begin to show the nature and extent of the problem. These narratives will be developed from the professional reflective journals of the writers and will assist in making the *'familiar strange and the strange familiar'* (Clough, 2002, p. 8). This will offer the reader an opportunity to capture the emotive aspects of the material, maintaining the contextuality, detail and richness (Thompson and Barnett, 1997). Each chapter includes the author's personal 'Practical Suggestions'. This emphasises the individual approach to student pastoral support that is evident in the research, and which is the underlying focus of the book.

● Ethics

Gabbard and Topeka (2000) argue that the use of clinical material for educational purposes or for publication presents the practitioner with a conflict of interest. A number of strategies can be used to deal with this dilemma, including disguise, consent, use of process rather than content and the use of composites. Students have a right to privacy that should not be infringed without informed consent. Identifying information should therefore not be published in written descriptions. Informed consent for this purpose requires that the subject be shown the manuscript to be published.

The author needs to make a judgement call about when a line is crossed and whether the disguise is potentially damaging to the educational credibility of the text. For example, if gender issues are pivotal to the issue, changing the gender will be out of the question. There is also the need to consider from whom one wishes to conceal the student's identity. Whilst attempting to conceal the identity from the student himself or herself is perhaps carrying disguise to an extreme, it would be appropriate to achieve it in relation to the student's peers and tutors. The authors in this book have therefore adopted this approach for their presentation of case studies.

● Exemplar

I have found myself increasingly reliant on my skills as a counsellor to manage the concerns that students such as Leanne bring. Her case study raises many of the key issues discussed in this book. It highlights the importance of positive relationships with personal tutors formed as early as possible in the course, and the importance of partnership with other support services within the institution. It shows the range and complexity of issues that tutors might be called upon to engage with and considers the potential consequences of inadequate support and the effect on student retention.

Case Study

The course content opened up a whole can of worms for me, sparking links to issues that I never realised I had been suppressing for more than 20 years. I could not possibly have imagined that I would have been affected so intensely by the reading that we were given. It deals with sexual abuse and the mental health issues this raises, and how people cope with their situation. I had not been a victim of this type of abuse, neither had my sister, but she has been physically and mentally abused for more than 20 years, by her husband, and he has mentally abused the children for many years. I have always been there to pick up the pieces and tried so hard to help her see that she had choices and could escape from her situation. I also tried to help her see that her son desperately needed professional help, mentally, all to no avail.

The reading had words that triggered links for me to my own situation. 'Abuse', 'mental health', 'inner voices', but the word that hit hardest was 'secrets', as my sister's children are encouraged to keep secrets from their father all the time in order to avoid his anger. Coupled with a documentary on domestic violence on television that night, the links in my mind were completed. I was suddenly overcome by an overwhelming, raw grief that hit me like a sledgehammer. I can only equate it with when my father died, it felt the same. Although the reading ended with the abused woman confronting her father and becoming empowered, it made me finally realise that nothing would ever change for my sister, that I was powerless to help her. This is why I felt I was grieving. My mind had been opened to the realisation that I was no different from my sister; I had also been in denial about her situation. To discover that I had repressed it for so many years was hideous and shocking, as I had always felt that I dealt with things. I cried constantly for a week, couldn't eat or sleep. I had palpitations and could barely put an intelligent thought together. Trying to function in seminars was virtually impossible. It was as though I had shut down completely in an act of self-preservation.

The following week I was to give a presentation on the subject. This was impossible, as I could not speak without crying. I forced myself to go to the seminar, as I did not want to give in to my feelings, but it was an ordeal. I felt nauseous and my heart was pounding. Listening to others in the group made me want to scream at how flippantly and trivially they seemed to treat the subject matter.

As a result of my experiences I became very withdrawn from the course and contemplated leaving but felt unable to contact my personal tutor as earlier approaches had been met with little warmth or

---

Case Study (*cont*)

interest. However, I eventually confided in a module tutor who was understanding and helpful. She listened and made me feel that it was worth trying to sort things out and then helped me to access the Counselling Service.

My feelings were still very close to the surface for some weeks. I started to feel more in control after some sessions with the Counsellor, who gave me some coping strategies. However, several months on I still feel very anxious about many things that would not have bothered me before this. I cannot cope with other people's problems, particularly if they are similar to my sister's, and I feel cold and detached, no longer able to be supportive to other people. I have to look after myself first.

I feel I have been forced to deal with issues, and I know that it is good that these things have come out into the open, but I strongly believe that if I had known in advance what issues were to be covered in the module I would have thought seriously about whether I would want to study that module, or at least have spoken to the tutor about the material it covered. If I had developed an earlier positive relationship with my personal tutor I might have accessed some support at an earlier stage which may have minimised my distress.

Although the exemplar given here brings up a number of serious issues that the personal tutor may be called upon to engage with, hopefully these will be in the minority in the workload of most personal tutors. However, it has been included here to demonstrate the potential seriousness of the subject matter and the interrelatedness of academic work with personal issues. When we first meet our personal tutees we can have no idea of their past experiences or triggers. Therefore I feel that the best that I can offer my tutees is the creation of a safe, ongoing relationship in which the students might express their concerns and ask for help when appropriate. This needs to be achieved without compromising the student's independent learning. I hope that the chapters within this book will explore ways in which this can be accomplished.

2 Overview of the Literature

Lindsey Neville

● Introduction

A search of the literature on personal tutoring revealed that key texts were mostly written in the late 1980s to early 1990s. Relevant literature therefore pre-dates the government 'widening participation' agenda in HE. All of the available literature acknowledges the importance of the role to the potential success or failure of individual students. Most United Kingdom (UK) universities have some variant of the personal tutoring system in place to support students.

● The role of the personal tutor

Although students may talk to admissions staff prior to beginning university, the personal tutor is usually a student's first personal contact with the university. They are the university's representative, from whom the student can receive academic and pastoral support. The personal tutor will either offer guidance and information directly or signpost the student to more specialist services. They are part of a network of services within higher education institutions intended to support students (Wheeler and Birtle 1993). Academic regulations usually confer this responsibility for both the personal and academic welfare of tutees onto the personal tutor, and highlight that the establishment of an effective partnership between Student Services and personal tutors is essential for effective student support. Race (2001) highlights the difficulty in seeing a clear dividing line between academic tutorials, which concern the subject being studied, and personal tutorials, which are concerned with the development of the whole student.

Personal tutors undertake a wide variety of roles with their students. This will depend upon the differing needs of their students, the requirements of the institution and the experience of the member of staff. Wheeler and Birtle (1993) highlight a number of these functions:

- Listener
- Confidante
- Advocate
- Disciplinarian
- Counsellor
- Careers adviser
- Teacher
- Mentor
- Assessor
- Adviser
- Referee

Lago and Shipton (1994) cite three main reasons for students to access personal tutor support, 'All of which can be seen as crossing the divide between the academic and the personal, "they come because they have been sent for, because they need support and advice or to rejoice"' (p. 96). The importance of 'knowing, tracking and supporting' (Owen, 2002, p. 7) each student has become an essential part of the role of the personal tutor. S/he has a central part to play in assisting students to fulfil the requirements of the course.

In most institutions this 'knowing, tracking and supporting' is achieved through a variant of the personal tutor system. Jaques (1989) suggests that the 'very existence of a personal tutoring system can give students the sense that they are cared about in what might otherwise seem a complex and impersonal system' (p. 6).

Higher education (HE) institutions therefore usually assign an academic member of staff to each undergraduate and postgraduate student. Their role is generally to provide pastoral guidance and support throughout the student's university life. This role may also include a responsibility for personal development planning (PDP) though this may occasionally be invested in a relationship with another academic member of staff.

● National context

The government target is that 50 per cent of young people under the age of 30 will have access to higher education by 2010. Consequently, there is a 'growing diversity of students in higher education with a growing number of mature entrants, part-timers and women students' (Dearing, 1997, p. 5).

The Higher Education Quality Council (HEQC) (Higher Education Quality Unit, 1996) highlights the impact of this diversity amongst the student population, on personal tutors. For example, older students were found to have increased levels of deliberate self harm and suicide, with students over 30 being overrepresented among referrals to student psychiatric services (O'Mahoney and O'Brien, 1980). This may, in turn, place increased demands for support onto the personal tutor. Students may also have no prior experience of traditional study methods and may have a variety of other commitments including caring responsibilities and part-time work (Owen, 2002).

Statistics for non-continuation of a first year higher education qualification show that 17 per cent of students in 2003/04 did not progress to the second year. Mature students had a higher non-continuation rate (14.2 per cent) than young entrants (12.3 per cent). These statistics do not include any students who left before 1st December in their first year of study (Higher Education Statistics Agency [HESA], 2006). Roberts et al. (2003) discuss the finding that non-traditional students, i.e. those from lower socio-economic backgrounds, are more prone to withdrawal than those from more traditional backgrounds. Consequently, those institutions with a high proportion of these students are more likely to have higher non-continuation rates.

A study at Hull University (Universities UK, 2002c) found that mature students were more likely to have considered withdrawing from university in the early stages of the course. Their recent appointment of Mature Students' Advisers seeks to provide support specifically for mature students through facilitation and co-ordination. Similar projects have been developed to provide services such as peer support through the buddying group. There is also a need for the support provided by higher education institutions (HEI) to be culturally relevant, ensuring that all services take into account religious, cultural and racial needs.

● Institutional context

Universities and colleges have a 'duty of care' to their students but they are not deemed to be *in loco parentis*. The legal framework with reference to HE institutions includes legislation on disability discrimination, health and safety, race equality, human rights and more recently, freedom of information. These issues are addressed more fully in other chapters.

Alongside this evolving legislative framework, Universities UK (2002c) highlights the moral duty of institutions to minimise potential risks to their student population. This perhaps needs to be seen in conjunction with the predominantly adult nature of the student body. The infrastructure within a university or college will therefore be instrumental in the development of student support and guidance systems. Recent developments in the provision of student support and guidance mechanisms have been effective in integrating the variety of support services under a centralised support service (Universities UK, 2002c). This increases the likelihood of recognising and monitoring students in distress. The same research accepts the importance of the links with front line academic staff, who are likely to be the first people to notice a student in distress. Their regular contact with the student might make it possible for them to detect changes in appearance or behaviour. Similarly, prolonged absence may be an indicator of distress.

The potentially contentious issue of confidentiality may compromise this relationship. Data protection legislation affords individuals privacy in respect of personal information and this may cause conflict in the sharing of relevant information between professionals within institutions. The usefulness of this front line service may be further compromised by the changes in course structure to a more modular system. This approach means that students are not necessarily having prolonged or regular contact with specific members of staff. Rivis (1996) and McNair (1997) have commented on the overstretching of the tutorial system for those institutions that have modularised their courses. This is seen as being partly because of increased student numbers, but also due to the drive towards greater efficiency and economic accountability.

These systems range from the explicit and constructed systems (Lago and Shipton, 1994) and the curriculum model (Brooman, 2002), where the role of the personal tutor is embedded within the working practices of the department, to the alternative more informal model adopted by many modular schemes. Several studies (Wheeler and Birtle, 1993; Owen, 1994, Rickinson and Rutherford, 1995) identify students' positive regard for a system which links personal tutor with academic study.

● The importance of the personal tutor

Rickinson and Rutherford (1995) identified that the majority of students who withdrew from university consulted their tutors for advice before they abandoned their studies. This highlights the importance of the role of the tutor in student retention. Higher education literature (Curtis and Curtis, 1966; and Rickinson and Rutherford, 1995) recognises the importance of the first year experience for student retention, and the need to understand how unsettling the transition from school to university can be. All have recognised the particular vulnerability of higher education students in their first year of study.

Grant (2002) showed that students were more likely to seek help and support from tutors than from any other institutional support provider. Students highlight that the availability of this support, together with approachability, are the key features of a successful relationship with personal tutors (Owen, 1994). However, recent changes within institutions may compromise the availability of that support.

> Academic and pastoral support from staff may be more difficult to access now, however, as a result of increasing student numbers without commensurate staff increases, the trend towards modular courses and the demand on academic staff for research and publications.   (Royal College of Psychiatrists [RCP], 2003, p. 11)

Owen (2002) identified a difference in the needs of home and residential students. Student participants felt that those students living away from home had a much greater need for the support, whilst 'home students' could rely on the existing support of family and friends. Persaud (2001) suggests that the majority of people in distress turn to informal rather than formal methods of help. Those who use these informal methods do not appear to go on to seek professional help. Personal tutors therefore appear ideally placed to make appropriate interventions that may benefit the students. The quality of the relationship with the personal tutor may be what will determine the effectiveness of the interventions.

● Student distress

Implicit in the role of lecturer in a higher education setting is the expectation that staff will give 'time and attention to students in distress', (Easton and Van Laar, 1995). The consideration of support for students in higher education necessitates an acknowledgement that learners are all at different stages of their lives. This will have an impact upon their expectation and use of the tutorial system. Students as a body are, by definition, a population in transition. They come into higher education for a limited time before moving on. As 'processes of transition are both exciting and stressful' (Lago and Shipton, 1994), all tutor relationships with students will offer tremendous potential for the expression of personal distress.

Easton and Van Laar (1995) identified a very high incidence (97 per cent) of lecturers being called upon to help distressed students – 32 per cent of the staff questioned felt that the number of students seeking help from personal tutors had increased. They reported that almost all of the staff in their study had dealt with at least one distressed student in the previous twelve months and that although they described their intervention as 'counselling', very few of them had any training in counselling.

University of Leicester (2002), in their research of students' help-seeking behaviour, found that 59 per cent of students had sought the help of their personal tutor when they were distressed. The same research study, amongst the staff, found that 52 per cent of the staff had supported students who in their opinion had a psychological or mental health problem. Only 15 per cent of the staff had attended any training to help them address the needs of students who may have psychological or mental health problems.

A report on the impact of increasing levels of psychological disturbance amongst students in higher education (Heads University Counselling Services, 1999) identified a lack of recognition on the part of the Department for Employment and Education (DFEE) of the resource implications of widening access to higher education for those from socially disadvantaged groups. This has particular significance in the light of the report of the Department of Health (DoH) (1998) highlighting the evidence of increased poor mental health amongst socially disadvantaged young people. There are similar links (Roberts et al., 2000) between poor student financing and psychological ill health. In 2002 Roberts expanded on the work further by identifying that one in four students admitted that they were in financial difficulty, and establishing clear links between financial problems and debt, and mental and physical ill health. 'There can be no doubt that this kind of lifestyle, fuelled by mounting debt, contributes to stress and ill-health' (Roberts, 2002). The work of Hodges and Smith, also in 2002, found that 50 per cent of students admitted experiencing more stress since starting at university, and that three-quarters are in debt.

Stanley and Manthorpe (2002) emphasise the potential tragic consequences of inadequate support for students in the light of the higher suicide statistics for young people generally and students specifically. In this research of parents of students who have committed suicide, contact with a personal tutor is seen as a key strategy in enlarging the safety net around students from the very beginning of their course. It is not seen as sufficient 'to leave it to people's good intentions' (p. 10). The need for adequate funding is seen as a crucial part of developing and maintaining pastoral responsibility.

● Student mental health

The World Health Organisation (WHO) report (2001) found that four out of the ten most disabling conditions in the world were types of mental illness. With an estimation of one in four adults experiencing a mental health problem in their lifetime, together with the economic and social changes which are linked to poor mental health (Patel, 2003), it is likely that widening participation in higher education institutions will increase the range of difficulties experienced by students.

Roberts (2002) identifies that compared with non students of the same age and gender, students were found to have poorer mental health. There are clearly implications for society generally and higher education specifically, where an increased proportion of its members may experience poorer mental health.

An increased awareness of mental health concerns and an increase in the proportion of depressive and suicidal behaviours (Samaritans, 1998) further affects the potential work of the personal tutor. The annual survey undertaken by the Association of University College Counsellors (AUCC), which collects data on the state of counselling in further and higher education, reports a steady increase in the proportion of seriously disturbed students since 1995–6. A recent study of students at the University of Leicester found that 40 per cent were very worried by coping with sadness, depression or mood changes.

The RCP (Royal College of Psychiatrists, 2003) supports the AUCC (1999) in its identification of an increase in the number of students experiencing mental health problems. Both attribute the rise to a general increase in mental health concerns in young people generally. Neither source appears to consider that an alternative or contributory explanation might be that there appears to be an increased awareness and acceptance of mental health issues amongst the population, evidenced by media coverage, which may prompt sufferers to seek support. The provisions required by the Disability Discrimination Act 1995 may also have contributed to a greater willingness on the part of students to declare a mental health disability. However, the AUCC (1999) suggests that the 0.12 per cent of the 1.6 million students in higher education who declared a mental health disability is a 'gross under representation'. This raises concerns about the institution's ability to fulfil its duty of care to the students, which can only be discharged if students declare their disability, ideally at admission.

A study by the RCP (2003) suggests that both academic staff and students have raised concerns about the mental health of students. Although the report highlights that 'vulnerable students might need higher levels of support in order to achieve their potential' (RCP, 2003, p. 11), none of the sixteen recommendations of the report highlight a potential role for academic staff in contributing to the amelioration of student difficulty. The emphasis is placed upon the role of mental health care advisers who are appropriately trained.

● Support for the tutor

Those who work with students in a therapeutic context have a variety of professional consultation, supervision and support mechanisms available to them. Few of these are likely to be available on a regular basis for the personal tutor. Student Services may provide workshops designed to support staff dealing with students in distress, and individual staff can usually make contact with Student Support Services for further advice and support as necessary and appropriate.

Cook et al., (1984) emphasise the range of problem areas, which may necessitate adept reactions from academic staff, and draw them into issues that are beyond their skills or training. Staff may then experience 'burnout' if they feel that they are not able to provide the help that students need (Maslach and Jackson, 1981).

Lomax (2004) acknowledges the impact of the university staff's role in supporting distressed students, with the development of a model to facilitate consideration of the helper's need for support. Whilst Universities UK (2002c) highlight the importance of providing support for Student Services staff in coping with the emotionally demanding work; there is no similar recognition of the impact on personal tutors of their work with the same students. Academic staff may also be supporting students who will not agree to a referral to counselling services or mental health advisers.

● Staff training

Ratigan (1986) found that research into tutor training and specifically counselling skills was limited. However, Lomax (2004) evidences training workshops for personal tutors from the 1980s onwards. Stanley and Manthorpe, (2002) highlight the importance of personal tutors in providing front line support for students with mental health problems. The importance of training and access to consultation is identified. Key conclusions of the study include the importance of enabling students rather than acting on their behalf, and the poor outcomes for staff who exceed their personal limitations. Research at two HE institutions found that the majority of staff wanted to help students as much as possible with their pastoral needs, but they voiced concerns about the lack of clarity around role expectations and the limited time available to offer the necessary level of support Heads of University Counseling Services [HUCS], 2003).

HUCS, 2003 found that 86 per cent of university counselling services offered training in mental health issues to non-clinical staff. Owen (2002) found that many tutors felt that there was no need for any kind of training in personal tutoring. It was seen as a natural skill inherent within those who were attracted to a career in lecturing.

● Progress files

Progress files form part of the new policy structure developed to ensure that outcomes in higher education are more explicit (Quality Assurance Agency, 2001). They are based on a recommendation of the National Committee of Inquiry in Higher Education and *'should consist of two elements: a transcript recording student achievement which should follow a common format devised by institutions collectively through their representative bodies; a means by which students can monitor, build and reflect upon their personal development'* (Dearing, 1997).

Transcript
The transcript element of the progress file is an institutional record of learning and achievement for each individual student. Individual institutions can choose how the information is presented but it should chart:

- what was studied;
- what was successfully completed;
- what was not successfully completed.

QAA (2001), *Guidelines for HE Progress Files*, includes a recommended data set for transcripts.

Personal Development Planning [PDP]
PDP is the element of their progress files though which students can *'monitor, build and reflect upon their personal development'*. It is a *'structured and supported process undertaken by an individual to reflect upon their own learning, performance and/or achievement and to plan for their personal, educational and career development'* (QAA, 2001, p. 2).

Different approaches have been developed to enable universities to meet the QAA expectations that all students will undertake personal development planning throughout their time at university. In some universities PDP has been embedded within the curriculum; other institutions have chosen to align it to the personal tutor system.

In 2003, Cottrell suggested that PDP was still a 'mutable entity'. At the time of writing (2007), this still seems to be the case. Anecdotal evidence from a number of universities suggests the student take-up has been very low. Part II of this book highlights the confusion that surrounds PDP for both staff and students. As not all higher education institutions have tied PDP to their personal tutoring it has not bee allocated a separate chapter in this book. However, it should be noted that the QAA (2001) suggests that PDP will help academic staff *'improve the quality of experience for tutors and tutees when it is linked to personal tutoring systems'* (p. 10).

● Conclusion

Providing both academic and pastoral support makes it 'difficult to define where tutoring and lecturing end and where counselling starts' (Lago and Shipton, 1994, p. 8). There is a need to draw a distinction between counselling and supporting, as the boundaries have become increasingly blurred. Race (2001) also discusses the difficulty in seeing a clear dividing line between academic tutorials and personal tutorials. The reality is that where both of these roles are invested in the same person there is no dividing line. In the modern world of HE the personal tutor must usually manage both, alongside each other, making it a task that may inevitably bring conflicts.

● Further reading

Cottrell, S. (2003), *Skills for Success: The Personal Development Planning Handbook* (Basingstoke: Palgrave Macmillan).

QAA (2001), *Guidelines for HE Progress Files*; see www.qaa.ac.uk/academic infrastructure/progressfiles/guidelines/profile2007.asp; (accessed 20 February 2007).

Thomas, L. (2006), 'Widening Participation and the Increased Need for Personal Tutoring', in L. Thomas and P. Hixenbaugh (eds), *Personal Tutoring in Higher Education* (Stoke on Trent: Trentham Books).

Part Two

Personal Experiences

3 Tutors' Experiences of their Role

Lindsey Neville

> This chapter will present the tutor's experience of the personal tutor role. It is evidence-based, using the experiences of personal tutors at the University of Worcester, through worked exemplars.

● Introduction

The University of Worcester is the only HE institution in Herefordshire and Worcestershire. In 2004–5 there were 7,596 students, with approximately 80 per cent studying on an undergraduate course. Approximately 19 per cent of students were on taught postgraduate programmes and just over 1 per cent were postgraduate research students. 60 per cent of the student population were mature and 7 per cent of the total student population had declared disabilities. This is slightly more than the national average of 5.5 per cent. The university employs over 650 staff (University College Worcester, 2005).

The aim of the research was to help the reader better understand the world of personal tutors and tutees and to highlight the different and often opposing needs of staff and students. As the founder of person-centred counselling, Carl Rogers developed a three-stage model which is useful in working in a helping context. In applying the Rogers (1967) model to a personal tutoring context, the understanding stage of the process is used cautiously and carefully to help the reader to understand the feelings and situations associated with personal tutoring. Used in this context it is hoped that the narratives presented will represent that which may be unconscious in the world of personal tutoring, and bring it into the conscious.

Within the research at the University of Worcester three clear threads of consistency, clarity and commitment emerged, which characterised the personal tutor's response to their role. Within these threads a number of issues are explored which have an impact on the work of the personal tutor.

● Consistency

The term 'consistency' is used to discuss both the changes perceived in student support and the variety of models of personal tutoring used across institutions to facilitate that support.

Models of personal tutoring

The lack of a consistent model of personal tutoring is a source of concern for many colleagues. Confusion is caused by having personal tutees on different courses, using different models of personal tutoring. This is particularly challenging during the early years as a personal tutor, when there is a great deal to learn about the structure of your own course without having to embrace the uncertainties of those courses that are constructed differently. Staff with little experience in tutoring in higher education were particularly confused by the different tutoring models. 'When I first arrived I had no idea what I was supposed to do' is typical of the comments received from those newer to the role. Even the more experienced colleagues were challenged by the sheer weight of paperwork where a variety of different models were used across one department.

Insights

I find it really difficult to remember what I have to do with each different group of students. I need to remember different protocols, different processes, different paperwork and different deadlines. It seems so unnecessary and I can't believe that it's impossible to organise it so that one tutor has similar groups of students. When a student asks a question, I need to sort out – before I answer – which course they are on. Also, I think I could do more of my tutorial work on a group basis and create more of a group identity if we met together as a distinct group working in the same way.

Students might form closer relationships with people on their own course if they shared a personal tutor. This might address some of the concerns they raise about the difficulty of getting to know people in the early weeks and months. The disparate nature of a modular system means that it is difficult to get students to engage in group activities because they do not know each other. Being able to engender feelings of belonging in tutorials may reap rich rewards in the classroom.

Thomas (2006) reviews the variety of models and explores their strengths and weaknesses. Colleagues seeking to explore alternative models may find this helpful.

Levels of support

As personal tutors we are entrusted with supporting a diverse group of students who are embarking on a period of considerable change in their lives. They are beginning the process of combining academic study with a likely significant change in their personal circumstances. For some this will mean living away from home for the first time, for others a change in how they perceive themselves and how others perceive them. One of my personal students told me that beginning university offered her the opportunity 'to be who I want to be rather than the person that others expect me to be'. This apparent reinvention of self is possible with the fresh start that university offers to some students. Students are able to develop relationships with their peers and staff without preconceived expectations. This freedom from some of the constraints in their lives brings with it other responsibilities; a need to develop the skills required to live and study with peers, work to deadlines, cope with the competing demands of caring or financial responsibilities and develop, extend or consolidate study skills. For many this may mean operating outside their comfort zone and without their usual support mechanisms.

These challenges for students require the provision, by institutions, of a robust system of support of which the personal tutor is usually the cornerstone. Personal tutors are therefore charged with supporting learning within potentially complex personal and social situations. They need to have an awareness of the impact of emotional distress on learning, to recognise that 'emotions of one kind – humiliation, fear, hesitancy – turn people off learning, create disruptions, feed into a sense of incompetence and self hatred' (Orbach, 2001, p. 4). This awareness of the impact of contributory factors in student learning highlights the importance of providing appropriate support. The integrity of the personal tutor system is therefore reliant on the skills of the individual tutors and the procedures which underpin it.

Since widening participation in 1992 ensured the entry of a diverse student population into many higher education institutions, expectations of the role of the personal tutor have changed. Today, this expectation requires that as tutors we accept responsibility for ensuring that the delivery of our lecture content is accessible to all. Additionally, there now appears to be a need and an implicit expectation that we ensure that our students are able emotionally to access their learning. Student stories highlight the potential impact of distress on their learning and these are explored in more depth in Chapter 4.

Increase in levels of support

Counsellors in new universities (Association of University College Counsellors [AUCC], 2005) have noticed an increase in the support that they need to offer students. Given that tutors are working with the same client group it is not unexpected that personal tutors, such as Ruth in the case study below, have also noticed an increase in the levels of support that they needed to provide.

Insights

The last five years have been particularly difficult as a personal tutor. I find myself needing to support students with a variety of issues that have never before impacted on the work to such an extent. Personal tutoring for me used to be about helping my students to maximise their grades. Now I feel it's about helping them to minimise the disruption in their studies caused by choices that they make in their personal lives.

It is almost inevitable that with the increase in student numbers institutions would see an increase in the number of students with mental health issues, particularly given the increased psychological problems in young people generally (Royal College of Psychiatrists, 2003).

Simon is a student in his early 30s. He was about ten years older than the average student in my personal tutorial group. In the early months he was a key figure in the group and helped a number of the younger students who were struggling to settle. Initially he seemed well organised and committed to his course. There appeared to be few problems in the first semester and he attended tutorials regularly. On one occasion a colleague mentioned that she thought that there was something 'not right' about his demeanour in the classroom but could not elaborate further. At tutorials I had noticed nothing unusual in his behaviour. In the second semester he joined one of my modules and I started to feel that his contributions were beginning to set him outside the group. He deliberately challenged people but could not construct an argument to support the challenge, leaving his peers bewildered. On one occasion his intervention with another student appeared hurtful and I tried to speak to him alone at the end of the session. Within seconds as I got closer to him it became clear by the smell that he had been drinking heavily. I hadn't experienced this kind of problem with a student before and decided that it would be wiser to arrange to speak to him when he was sober. We arranged a tutorial for the next day, when he appeared apologetic for his behaviour. He told me about an argument with his partner, which had upset him and resulted in the heavy drinking. I discussed with him the inadvisability of attending lectures in such a state and he offered to apologise to the student who he had upset. As we talked he told me that he wanted to put things right, as university was a new start for him. Throughout his life he had suffered from crippling periods of depression, often using alcohol as a way of coping, and that coming to university was part of his plan for addressing his personal difficulties. Despite his commitment to the course his work began to slide and other tutors began to tell me of problems in their lectures. His appearance became dishevelled and his attendance poor. Nothing I did or said seemed to make any difference and gradually he just faded away from the course and the university.

Simon is representative of a number of students who may see university as the answer to their problems. Additionally, Health and Social Care courses may sometimes seem to attract students who are looking for or need some care in their lives. He clearly valued his personal tutor and spoke with her or him freely, and I wonder whether s/he could have used his/her influence and good relationship to encourage him to seek professional help through a referral to a mental health adviser, GP or counsellor. Those who use alcohol or drugs can be unstable and the tutor needs to value his/her own safety. Challenging a student who could be volatile is risky, particularly as buildings can be deserted as soon as evening lectures end. Making a tutorial appointment for a time when you know others will be around is the safest option. Suspected substance abuse may also be reportable for students who are undertaking courses leading to professional registration, such as nursing.

This increased level of support, needed by many students, may have an impact on the well being of those required to provide it.

I find that the hardest situations to deal with are those where I feel powerless to change difficult circumstances in my tutee's life. I have one tutee whose personal situation is heart rending. Mia succeeded in gaining a place at university despite the death of her mother when she was nine and the subsequent breakdown of family life and being placed in the care of social services. In the first year, when others looked forward to visits home and contact from their families in the early difficult months of transition and adjustment, she was isolated and alone. The first Christmas was a particularly difficult time for her. Her situation brought home to me the importance of support for students if they are to maximise their potential. Once I realised her personal circumstances I spent tutorial time with her, mostly just showing an interest in her and her work. There were times when I feared that the absence of family support would render her unable to continue with the course. Her lowest time was when a relationship that had predated her move to university broke down. She became very distressed and withdrawn. It was at this time that I became aware that Mia had a history of self harm and that during difficult periods she cut her arms as a way of coping with or expressing her feelings. In one meeting she told me that she 'couldn't go on any longer'. I asked her what she meant and she said that 'everything was too hard'. I tried to encourage her to see the counsellor but she insisted that no-one could help, and would not agree to a referral to the university counsellor.

Amazingly, she has stayed on the course and is now in the third year. There have been difficulties for her in developing and maintaining relationships with her peers and so I shared her joy when a small group of fellow students asked her to flat share with them. She was much more adept with her relationships with adults which she attributes to being 'looked after'.

The challenge for me was to offer appropriate support, avoiding trying to replace everything that she has lost. It was all made harder because I liked her enormously and she was the same age as my own daughter and I was often very close to inviting her into my home and family. There are times when working with her has left me feeling overwhelmingly sad.

It is compelling to want to make the world a better place for students such as Mia, but the tutor here rightly identifies that her hardest challenge was to maintain appropriate boundaries. The unique nature of the relationship between personal tutor and student can make these boundaries difficult to judge. Expectations of both student and tutor will vary with individual circumstances and experiences. It is important to think about the message that your behaviour will give to the student if, for example, you give out your home or mobile telephone number, lend a student money or invite them to your home. The key is to decide what feels appropriate to you and that you recognise the potential consequences of breaching any of these boundaries that you put in place.

Another key issue for this tutor was that of possible student suicide, which is traumatic for all concerned and obviously a most distressing subject for the tutor to have to confront. It is important for tutors to recognise that the personal tutoring relationship is not necessarily a confidential one as most tutors are not working within a professional code of ethics. It is always preferable to get the students' permission to discuss them with someone else. However, in the case of a possible student suicide, it is perhaps more important to try and ensure the student's safety than to maintain confidentiality. Students that I have spoken to, regarding referral, have been fearful about speaking to someone that they do not know. The tutor will need to hear and acknowledge these concerns and try to reassure the student about the approachability of the referral agency.

A student's tendency to self harm as a way of coping with, and expressing feelings will be alarming for the personal tutor. Understanding more about self harming may help tutors to work with the student and refer them appropriately:

- The majority of young people who self harm are between the ages of 12 and 25.
- Incidence declines after 25.
- Those affected by the cycle of self harm can recover.
- Four times as many females as males are affected.
- Self harm can lead to suicide but the majority of those affected are not trying to kill themselves.

(Camelot Foundation and Mental Health Foundation, 2006)

Many universities have responded to the increase in the severity of presenting distress in students by appointing mental health advisers, who are qualified mental health nurses. They can offer confidential opportunities for students experiencing mental health difficulties to receive support. Ongoing support can be provided for students with longer-term problems if necessary. Both counselling and mental health services will usually provide staff with advice if they are concerned for a student's well being. However, unless you are concerned for the safety of the student, as in the case of Mia, the reality is that students are free to decide for themselves whether or not to seek additional support.

These case studies highlight the recognition, amongst staff with considerable experience in the role, that the changes in higher education in recent years have brought about acceleration in the needs of their students.

● Clarity

Clarity was expressed in the research through what might be described as boundary issues or limits applied to the scope of the work. Reasons given for applying limits to the work include gender, lack of aptitude or interest in the work, and concern about operating outside levels of expertise.

Boundaries

There is clearly an ongoing debate amongst lecturers in higher education as to the appropriateness of the role of a personal tutor, with opinions ranging from discontent at any involvement at all, to finding it to be one of the most rewarding aspects of their work. There is also recognition of the difficulties posed by the conflicts between personal and academic support. Such opinions include:

- I enjoy the research and teaching in my role but for many reasons I feel very uncomfortable about being a personal tutor. As a man I don't want to put myself in the position where young women might confide personal issues. It's just not what I thought I had signed up for. I feel very uncomfortable and vulnerable. If a student brings a personal concern to me I just tell them to see the counsellor – that's what they are for.
- I don't want to be a social worker!
- I don't think I am any good at listening to people's problems.
- I am confused about the limits of my role as a personal tutor. Further training to define this would be helpful.
- I don't really know what is expected of me.

Range of issues presented by students

Understanding the range of issues that are presented within personal tutorials is key to comprehending the boundaries within which the tutorial should sit. From the student focus group a range of academic and personal issues were identified. These were included within both staff and student questionnaires to identify a combined priority listing, as set out in Table 1.1 Students and staff show some consistency in the use made of personal tutorials. Academic progress, study skills, stress and learning difficulties are indicated as the key areas (by aggregate scoring) that personal tutors are expected to provide at least initial support for.

Table 1.1   Key issues for tutorial's aggregate position

Both students and staff were asked to indicate which of a number of different issues they had discussed within tutorials.

Aggregate positon	Student position	Staff position
Academic progress	1	1
Study skills	2	1
Stress	3	4
Learning difficulties	6	4
Careers	3	8
Unhappiness	5	7
Relationships	9	3
Bereavement	7	6
Accommodation	8	10
Depression	12	9
Finance	10	11
Loneliness	10	13
Homesickness	13	12

When discussing the results of this research with colleagues the response to the prevalence of stress within personal tutorials was a cause for concern, as it was felt that they themselves were struggling to cope with the stress of their work, leaving them ill-equipped to support students with similar concerns. One tutor described a tutorial with one of her tutees which had compounded her own stress.

> The student had come to see me to seek help in overcoming the stress that she felt was threatening to disrupt her studies. She was juggling the care of both teenagers and elderly parents, trying to meet assignment deadlines and maintaining a relationship with her partner. Her partner appeared to be struggling with the changes that had been brought about by her studies. Priorities had shifted in the home and there was now little time for them as a couple. Things that they used to do together were now done separately. As she spoke of the difficulties that she was facing I became aware that I was trying to manage many of the same things and, on top of that, now felt that I had to try to provide support for the student. I realised that I was not coping with my own stress. I have no real recollection of what I said during the tutorial. All I can remember is a sense of panic and a tightening in my chest. I felt unable to help myself let alone the student. This tutorial triggered an awareness within me of all that was causing me concern in my own life. All of it suddenly seemed to be unmanageable. I couldn't see a way through my own difficulties. I felt overwhelmed. I continued to cope reasonably well with other aspects of the work but couldn't face being alone with a student. I feared what they would tell me and was concerned that the anxiety I felt would be apparent to others. I was loathe to admit to colleagues that I couldn't cope and eventually went to my GP, who diagnosed stress and signed me off work. I felt such a failure but knew that I couldn't put myself back in a position where I might be exposed to the troubles of my students when I couldn't cope with my own.

Although the key issues for tutorials, raised by both staff and students, related to academic matters, case studies revealed that other personal issues inevitably arose as a result of the presenting issues. These wide-ranging academic, emotive and personal-development arenas indicate a demand on personal tutors that may fall outside their skills and experience. Many are unrecognised in the selection and appointment criteria for academic staff.

Commitment

Commitment was expressed within the research, both in terms of what the institution might do to facilitate the improvement of the personal tutoring system, and regarding the personal commitment to the role on the part of the staff involved. This involves exploring issues such as the importance of the role, practical considerations which affect the role, together with continuing professional development. It also addresses the importance of institutional commitment to promoting and supporting the well being of personal tutors, who may deal with difficult and complex personal and social issues.

Importance of the role

Of those personal tutors questioned, 92 per cent viewed the role as very important. Comments about the importance of the role revealed:

> - It's one of my favourite aspects of the work.
> - Sometimes I feel that by listening I can make a difference.
> - Listening to students' concerns helps me to understand them better.

Practical considerations

Staff were asked to consider practical issues which might have an impact on work with students. Three key areas were identified:

- sharing office space;
- pressures of other aspects of the work (no further breakdown was pursued);
- number of personal students.

This view of the importance of privacy is highlighted by case studies. There were a number of examples of personal tutors wandering the corridors with distressed students, looking for somewhere to talk.

Insights

I share an office with a colleague. Most of the time there is no problem, we like working together. It does become very difficult when students want to speak in confidence about a personal matter. One of my personal students turned up unannounced, she seemed very upset and asked if she could speak to me. It obviously wasn't appropriate for us to use the office and we spent the next 20 minutes wandering the corridors looking for somewhere to go. I was embarrassed. It didn't look very professional.

Pressure of work
The conflicting demands of other aspects of the work were another concern for some staff.

Insights

*It can be difficult to create opportunities to meet with my
personal tutees which fit with both their schedule and mine.
Timetabled sessions would help to alleviate the problem. It
might also create greater equality of opportunity in the accessing of support as it would combat the current system where no
time is allocated and the work sinks to the lowest point on my
'to do' list.*

Although staff acknowledged the value of effective personal tutoring,
there was concern about the time that it takes to do this well.

Insights

*I am aware that, because I don't see my tutees that often, I need
to reconnect with them each time I see them before moving on
to the business of the tutorial. To establish and then maintain
an effective relationship I feel that I have to ask about their
families/accommodation/job/progress/existing problems that I
am aware of. This all takes time (more time than I ever account
for!). It means that I am often running late. On one occasion I
thought I was just going through the motions of this reconnect-
ing but as soon as I asked how the student was, she burst into
tears. She then started to tell me about a relationship breakdown. She had decided to break off the relationship because he
had started to become violent towards her. This had left her
feeling alone and vulnerable, so although it was I who had
asked to see her to verify her practice experience, it proved to be
an opportunity for some timely support.*

Methods of contact

A variety of methods were used for contact between personal tutors and
tutees:

- office telephone
- mobile phone
- text
- email
- drop in
- pre-booked appointments

Office Telephone

Telephone contact from personal tutees was viewed as problematic as it often necessitates leaving messages on a telephone system which is shared by three or four tutors. The reliability of this was questioned by many, particularly where part-time staff were involved and messages could sit on colleagues' desks for several days before they were next in the office.

Email

Some staff considered that the volume of emails which circulate makes it difficult to keep up with a reasonable response rate to students' requests, but this was juxtaposed with those who felt that the use of email to maintain contact with tutees was time-saving.

Insights

Group distribution lists are a real problem for me. I estimate that about half of the emails that I receive have no relevance at all to me. Unfortunately, I have to read them to find that out!

Insights

I find it difficult to keep in touch with my tutees and being part-time doesn't help. Last year I started a new system in which I email each of them at the beginning and end of each semester. I might wish them a Happy New Year or a good summer/Easter break and then go on to remind them how to get in touch if they need to. In some cases, for example where there is a course requirement for me to verify practice experience, I can also use the message to clarify what I expect of them. It's a very quick and easy way to feel that I have demonstrated some commitment to them. I have found that it also seems to encourage them to contact me by email rather than just dropping in which means I can organise my time more efficiently. One student who was feeling quite isolated early on in the first year told me that just seeing that I was trying to make a connection with her helped her to realise that she was not alone – there was someone that she could approach if she needed to.

Pre-booked appointments

Many departments require that staff have an appointment sheet on their office door which offers students the opportunity to sign up for a tutorial at a convenient time. There was criticism of this approach as personal tutors were frustrated at the time wasted when students failed to turn up at the appointed time.

Insights

I estimate that about a third of those who sign up on my door for tutorials don't turn up. This could be because the aim of pre-booking is to plan ahead but it seems to me that many of our students have been brought up in the age of mobile phones where arrangements are made more spontaneously. They are used to their needs being met immediately. Consequently, they make an appointment at the point of need but then the need passes before the scheduled appointment and so they don't turn up. I now try to have a drop-in session for half an hour twice a week and I find that this means that I waste less time.

Continuing professional development

Staff were well qualified for the work, with 85 per cent having undertaken some form of professional development in relation to personal tutoring: 39 per cent had counselling or counselling-skills qualifications; 32 per cent of staff had undertaken both counselling/counselling-skills qualifications and further professional development; 15 per cent of staff had undertaken no form of professional development in relation to personal tutoring. The professional development undertaken was highly regarded by those staff who had participated:

- The basic counselling course was excellent and really helped me.
- I have done several of the staff development courses and each time have come away with positive strategies and techniques that have really helped.

Its value in equipping personal tutors for the kind of complex issues they might face is exemplified by the support given to a student who had been raped.

A personal student confided in me that she had been raped. She was obviously very distressed and gradually told me the story. I was pleased that she felt able to speak to me. One of the issues that made it particularly difficult was my gender. I was very aware that she needed to trust me not only as her personal tutor but also as a man. Fortunately, I have some counselling training which enabled me to hear her story and ultimately refer her appropriately. At first she was resistant to going elsewhere, feeling that she couldn't face going through her whole story again. Initially she felt that all that she needed was to have spoken about what happened. Over time I was able to impress upon her the potential value of taking the opportunity to resolve some of the consequences of the rape that she was experiencing. Eventually she went to see the university counsellor, who was able to work through many of her feelings. Despite referring her I still saw her regularly and was able to support her with other aspects of university life whilst she worked on coming to terms with what had happened to her.

Impact on the personal tutor

Of those questioned, 85 per cent had occasionally worked with distressed students. 15 per cent had frequently worked with distressed students; 77 per cent were occasionally overwhelmed by the needs of their personal tutees; and 15 per cent were frequently overwhelmed. There was a recognition that working with distressed students affected their own well being.

Some time ago one of my second-year personal students came to see me for a progress tutorial. She said that she wanted some help with maximising her grades. I talked to her about her grade profile and the range of comments that she had received. She told me that she wanted to get the best possible degree classification. As we talked she became upset and tearful and eventually told me that she wanted to do well for her Dad. He had died shortly before she started at university. As she told me about him and why it was important to her I was aware that my feelings about the recent death of my own father were very close to the surface. I had tears in my eyes and felt at a loss to know what to do. I had to move away from the emotive aspects of the discussion in order to gather my composure. I did want her to know that I understood her pain but it didn't feel appropriate to cry in front of her. I was upset for some time afterwards as I felt I had let her down as I struggled to deal with my own grief.

Of staff respondents, 62 per cent felt equipped some of the time to support the students with the concerns that they bring; 38 per cent always felt equipped to deal with student concerns. Length of service had no effect on staff perception of their capacity to cope. Impact on the well being of the personal tutor was marginally increased for part-time staff. This could perhaps be because although they are exposed to fewer student concerns their part-time status means that the support of colleagues is less accessible to them.

Insights

Sometimes students get themselves into such messes that I feel we just go round and round in circles discussing every twist but nothing ever changes. It feels hopeless to try and help. I just need a magic wand! When I have seen this particular student I always go home feeling low.

Those who had not undertaken professional development were likely to feel less equipped to deal with student concerns.

Insights

I have to prioritise my workload and so I choose to put the emphasis on that which is discipline-related. I haven't under-taken any professional development designed to help me as a personal tutor. Students will, hopefully, seek out those who have a greater aptitude and interest in the role.

Support

Of those questioned, 85 per cent used colleagues as a support system for coping with personal tutor issues. This highlights the importance of mutual support systems which operate within departments, and the collegiate response to colleagues' concerns. Several staff expressed concern that these informal support systems were neither recognised nor formalised:

- More robust support systems are needed for staff, managed from within departments, rather than by the institution.
- Without the opportunity to discuss with colleagues some of the issues that students bring, I think I would struggle to cope.

Those who used the counselling service as a means of support were in the minority but the support offered to those tutors was highly valued.

- Support via the counselling service is excellent.
- Continue to offer support via the counselling service. Its support has been invaluable when I have been struggling with the concerns of my students.
- Sometimes I refer students to the counsellor but they don't always want to go, so I have sought guidance about how I can best help.

Practical suggestions

☐ Consider your personal boundaries in advance of forming relationships with students.

☐ Discuss difficult situations with the university counsellor or Student Services, keeping the student's anonymity.

☐ Ensure that you maintain your own sense of well being by using the support services available to you.

● Further reading

Camelot Foundation and Mental Health Foundation (2006), *The Truth about Self Harm*, www.mentalhealth.org.uk/publications/?EntryID=45371 (accessed 28 November 2006).

Heads of University Counselling Services (1999), *The Impact of Increasing Levels of Psychological Disturbance amongst Students in Higher Education*, www.rhbnc.ac.uk/~uhye099/hucsreport.html (accessed 23 March 2005).

Jaques, D. (1989), *Personal Tutoring* (Oxford: Oxford Centre for Staff Development).

Lago, C. and Shipton, G. (1994), *Personal Tutoring in Action* (Sheffield: University Counselling Service).

Thomas, L. and Hixenbaugh, P. (eds) (2006), *Personal Tutoring in Higher Education* (Stoke on Trent: Trentham Books).

Wheeler, S. and Birtle, J. (1993), *A Handbook for Personal Tutors* (Buckingham: Open University Press).

4 Students' Experiences of Personal Tutoring

Alexa Collicott and Lindsey Neville

This chapter is a collaboration between Alexa Collicott, who has experience of undergraduate and postgraduate distance learning at two different universities, and Lindsey Neville's research into students' experience of the undergraduate personal tutor system at the University of Worcester, in addition to her personal experience of both undergraduate and postgraduate learning. The aim is to present a range of student experiences of their personal tutor.

Introduction

The starting point for this collaboration was a comparison of our individual experiences of beginning university. The obvious difference in our experiences was the intervening 27 years.

Insights

My first experience of university took place in 2001, just before my 18th birthday. I had gained a place at a traditional university and intended to live in university student accommodation. I was allocated a place in a student flat sharing with five others. It quickly became apparent that all of the other students in the flat were mature students. Despite trying very hard to get to know people I struggled to cope with the first few days. Activities were arranged by the Students' Union but nothing was very structured. I realised very early on that I had a problem but at that time I didn't even know that I had a personal tutor. I tried to talk to someone from accommodation services but they were very unsympathetic about my situation. Over the next few days I realised that a great deal would have to change for me to settle and I feared that the response I had received might be typical of the support available to students. Consequently, I made the decision to leave.

The transition from school to college can be challenging for all young people. Leaving home for the first time, sharing accommodation with people outside the family, managing their own finances will all have an impact on the experience. This highlights the importance of all student services recognising the vulnerability of students at the beginning of their course. Students will also have decided on their future course and institution a year before they actually take up the place, so personal circumstances and interests may have changed. Therefore, the reasons for student withdrawal may not always be course- or institution-related. Johnston (2000), McGivney (1996) and National Audit Office (2002) recognise the significant part that social aspects such as isolation might play as contributory factors in early withdrawal rates. As we have seen, these early withdrawals are not included in HESA statistics.

Alexa's first experience of university highlights how quickly problems can occur and the speed with which students can then make negative judgements about their situation. This emphasises the need to put support systems in place from the time of the student's arrival rather than at the beginning of the course, which in some cases may be as much as two weeks later. These two weeks can therefore be seen as critical.

When Lindsey was first at college in 1974 many of the issues that Alexa faced were also apparent.

Insights

When I left home to begin my teacher training course in 1974 I struggled to cope with the changes that the move necessitated. For several months I remember being very unhappy and contemplated leaving. However, at that time institutions viewed themselves as being in 'loco parentis' and there were a number of people with responsibility for student welfare. This began with the house warden, who monitored how often we could go home for weekends, who our visitors were and how long they stayed. There was an evening curfew to ensure that staff always knew where we were. The hall of residence was also home to several academic staff, who ate with us and were there to address any problems. I recall one particular member of staff who took a great deal of time helping me to adjust. Another source of support throughout my course was my college 'mother'. This was a student in the year above whose role was to offer support and information from the moment that a place was accepted. Great care was taken to try and pair new

*students with someone from their home area so that meetings
could take place in the summer before starting at college.
Personal tutors were also very involved in our lives, and meetings with them were compulsory. I was never short of someone
to talk to about how I felt. Consequently, I weathered the initial
difficult months.*

Whilst it would be inappropriate to return to a time when young people
were viewed paternalistically by institutions, there are elements of the
support available then that would offer some protection for today's students.
Mentoring schemes do exist for current students but in some universities are
more focused on the needs of mature students.

Alexa decided to take a year out to work, and reapply for a place at a
different university the following year.

Insights

*After my previous experiences of university accommodation it
seemed safer to try again at a university closer to home where I
could continue to live with my parents. I successfully graduated
but my time at university was made easier because I didn't need
to rely on the university's support systems. I was able to retain
the support of all of my family and existing friends as well as
making new friends on my course. I also didn't need to worry
about money as I could return to the part-time job that I had
held for several years. Even though I didn't need the level of
support that I had previously, I was still aware that the early
days were the hardest and personal tutor meetings didn't take
place until several weeks into the course. I watched many
people from the course struggle to adjust to their new student
life; some didn't make it and left before the end of the first
semester.*

These stories suggest that it is individual staff members who can make a
difference in the students' transition to university when usual support mechanisms such as family and friends are temporarily unavailable. As the
cornerstone of university support systems, an exploration of the student
experience of personal tutoring is crucial if we are to deepen our understanding of the role.

● Undergraduate experiences of personal tutoring

A literature review, prior to the research with undergraduates at the University of Worcester, identified a number of key areas – availability, approachability and appropriateness – which typify what students feel is important in the relationship between personal tutor and student (Owen, 2002). The combined data from student questionnaires, focus groups and case studies was therefore sorted under these headings.

Availability

Availability was seen in terms of the expediency of the communications systems in use, methods of contact and communication, and students' immediate and urgent support needs.

Expediency

The inability to easily arrange a mutually convenient appointment was a key issue for many students. The conflicts of contemporary student issues such as pressures of paid employment and caring responsibilities were seen as contributory factors.

> - Difficulty in finding time due to work constraint.
> - Several of my modules run in the evening so that's when I am usually in, but I can obviously never get to see my tutor then.
> - It's difficult to get appointments that fit in with your timetable so I end up having to come in on another day. It costs about £10 in petrol every time I have to make an additional journey.
> - There is no timetable on his door – how am I supposed to make an arrangement?

Concerns were expressed about the difficulties which emerge when the student is studying part-time.

> - Part-time therefore not always available.
> - Part-time therefore restricted availability.
> - Last semester, the days when I was in for lectures were not the days that my part-time personal tutor worked.

These difficulties appear to be compounded for those who are part-time students with a part-time tutor.

Insights

I am part-time and so is my personal tutor (she is also my independent study tutor). It is really difficult to arrange meetings when she and I are both available. It seems madness to put us together. It creates a difficulty that just isn't necessary. I don't want to make a fuss because she may think it's because I don't like her. Its not that – it just makes life so difficult.

Contact and communication

A variety of methods were used by students to book tutorials, including telephone, email and booking through a timetable system on the office door. Many students expressed concern about the ease of making tutorial arrangements. Students felt that staff were poor at responding to both emails and telephone calls.

> - When I wanted to see my tutor earlier this semester I visited his office almost every day and never managed to find him in and there was no timetable on the door. I gave up visiting and tried email and the phone. Eventually after 2 weeks he returned an email – I had almost given up. I wonder what I would have done if the need had been urgent.
> - She never replies to my emails – I have given up.
> - It took me four weeks to get a tutorial with my personal tutor. He didn't respond to my emails or telephone calls.

In a focus group students felt that the tutorial system would be more effective if more efficient use was made of electronic communication. It was a significant factor in many of the interviews with students, who felt that many tutors did not make appropriate use of email to maintain regular contact with their tutees.

> - More use could be made of email to stay in touch.
> - My tutor sends me an email at the start and end of each semester. At least I know that she is aware that I exist, and it also reminds me that she is there for me if problems arise. Even if I don't have any other contact with her I feel OK about it.

Students are frustrated when they leave telephone messages for staff which are not answered in a timely fashion because the tutor was on study leave, sick leave, or part-time working and therefore not in for a few days.

Insights

*For some time I had been getting behind with my assignments.
If I am honest with myself I think I was having too good a time
with the social side of university life and just didn't take the
work seriously enough. I often didn't bother going to lectures at
all, particularly if they were in the morning. Once I had realised
that I had a problem and that I might not pass the first year it
started to worry me, but the worry didn't seem to push me into
doing anything and I just slipped further behind. It came to a
head after Easter when I should have done a mandatory presentation. I didn't turn up so eventually got a message from the
module tutor saying that I would fail the module. I began to
realise the seriousness of my situation and emailed my personal
tutor to ask for some help in planning how I could sort things
out. I didn't get a reply, so I went a few times to his office to try
and talk to him but he was never in. Meanwhile the problems
were getting worse. Finally, I went to the course administrator
to ask her to pass on a message, where I was told that my
personal tutor had been off sick for the last 2 months.*

Immediate and urgent support

Both staff and students felt that the need to always pre-plan tutorials created
a problem. Often the support needed was immediate and it was difficult to
find anyone to help. There were examples of students feeling that there was
no one for them to turn to.

- I thought about going to see the administrator when I was
  desperate for help but it always looks like we aren't
  supposed to go in there. I wouldn't know who to talk to.
- I received some very bad news from family by telephone and
  knew that I would have to go home for a while. I really
  wanted to talk to someone about what I was going to do. I
  went to see my personal tutor first, who wasn't in her office,
  and then tried every other course module tutor that I felt I
  could talk to. No one was available and I left university that
  day feeling upset about what had happened and wishing
  that I could have talked to someone then and there. I didn't
  know which way to turn, but I wouldn't have wanted to talk
  to a stranger.

- One of my personal students emailed me last year and asked to see me as soon as possible. With all of my other commitments it was 10 days before I had time to dedicate to her. When she arrived in my office she looked pale and drawn. I asked her how she was and what I could do to help. She simply said 'I just wanted you to know that my mum died'.

Approachability

The data suggested that approachability is discussed in terms of perspectives on the importance of the personal tutoring role and the number and quality of the interactions.

Importance of the personal tutor

The role of personal tutor was viewed by 70 per cent of students as very important or important. Students were more likely to view the role in this positive light if their own experience of the system had been positive. Several students commented that their personal tutor had been instrumental in actually keeping them on the course. The stories provided by student case studies emphasise the importance of the relationship between student and personal tutor in light of the impact of wider issues such as isolation, finance, accommodation and caring responsibilities faced by students.

Case Study

I dropped out of university in 2001 only five weeks into my life as a degree student. So, this is second time round for me. This time round I am finding things hard again. Tuition fees, petrol prices and the cost of text books mean that I need to work 30 hours a week to avoid getting into financial trouble. This makes it difficult to enjoy the social side of university. If you aren't involved socially it can lead to feeling isolated and alone. It's been very difficult but my personal tutor has been very understanding – I might have given up again by now if it hadn't been for his encouragement and support.

Case Study

In the middle of my second year I had a terrible time with one of the girls that I shared a house with. It really upset me. It went on for a long time and I found it difficult to concentrate on my work and started to get behind. My personal tutor really helped; she listened to how upset I was but also helped me make a plan for how I could still get all my assignments in. I couldn't have managed it without her. I think that the most important thing that she did was to 'be there'. I knew that if things got too much for me she would always try to make time for me. She made me feel that I mattered. I can't thank her enough.

Number of interactions

Of the student respondents, seven per cent had never seen their personal tutor; 65 per cent had seen their tutors between one and three times in the last academic year, with 26 per cent of students having attended between four and eight times. Being part-time was not a significant factor in the amount of contact with a personal tutor. With regard to age, twice as many 25+ students as 18–25's had not seen a personal tutor.

Quality of the interactions

A range of comments reflected the positive light in which many students viewed their interactions with their personal tutor.

- I don't think I could have kept going without her.
- She was always there for me.
- I might have given up by now if it hadn't been for her encouragement and support.

Of the sample, 22 per cent were less complimentary about the support that they had received from their personal tutor;. 15 per cent felt that their personal tutor had been unhelpful, with 7 per cent viewing the interaction as very unhelpful.

- Doesn't seem to have anything to say to me.
- My meetings have all been a waste of time.
- I don't think she knows what she is talking about.
- My personal tutor is virtually a stranger to me. She has never taught on any of my modules and I think she is part-time. If I had problems I don't know what I would do, but I

> certainly wouldn't feel comfortable about going to see her as she has been totally uninvolved with me so far. I am quite jealous when others speak of how good their tutors have been.

Some students felt rejected by their personal tutors. This was as a result of either a misunderstanding of roles or the lack of an early contact by the tutor.

> • When I have tried to make an appointment to see her in the past she has been away, and not responded for some time, or said she would contact me in a few days time to make an appointment, but never did.
> • I feel I have enough work to do without having to chase up my tutor to remind her of appointments. I therefore feel that I have not built up any relationship with her.

Opportunities for intervention appear to be minimised when positive relationships have not been established before problems arise. Several students commented that they did not meet their personal tutor until several weeks into the course.

> • I was so disappointed when I discovered that the person who was to be my personal tutor couldn't even turn up to meet me on day one.
> • Those of us whose personal tutors couldn't be bothered to turn up were just left to one side. I really envied those whose personal tutor was there.
> • My tutor never got in touch with me – so I didn't bother either.
> • From the very beginning I knew she was someone that I would go to if I needed someone to talk to.
> • She seemed to understand how awkward we might feel.

Some relationships were described as strained from the beginning and students were left feeling that they had been 'short changed' by the system. There was a lack of awareness that it was possible to change personal tutor.

- I found her very unwelcoming and unapproachable when I tried to arrange an appointment.
- I got the message that I was being a nuisance.
- I wish I could change my personal tutor. It feels as if he doesn't like me and I don't like him.
- I think that the allocation of personal tutor could be likened to that of the lottery (only a few people are lucky!). I have been really lucky with mine. Whenever I see her I get the feeling that she is pleased to see me and interested in the progress that I am making, but I have many friends who have not been so fortunate. I think liking your tutor is very important, I can think of module tutors who I wouldn't want as a personal tutor. I like mine and I think she likes me. I see her as something of a role model in how I would like to be as a professional.

The time available for tutorials impacted on the use that was made of them.

- My tutor always makes me feel like she has a train to catch in the next five minutes. It discourages me from speaking fully about anything.
- There never seems enough time to say everything I feel I need to say.

Appropriateness

The appropriateness of the personal support offered and received is expressed in terms of the boundaries which surround the role of personal tutor, together with the range of issues covered within tutorials. The consistency of the support received is a further matter for discussion.

Boundaries

There appeared to be some confusion surrounding the boundaries of the role of personal tutor. Many students said they had not realised that the personal tutor could be used for issues other than purely academic concerns.

- At no point did I consider speaking to my personal tutor because I have only met her on one occasion. Also, I had not realised that she was there to support me with personal issues; I thought she was just there to discuss academic progress. But, even if I had known that I could talk to her in such a way, I don't think I would have done. It would have felt too difficult to discuss anything personal with someone I hardly knew.

- Not entirely sure what I should discuss with my personal tutor.
- I felt I shouldn't be bothering her with my personal trivial problems.
- Helpful with academic issues but unhelpful with personal problems.

In one focus group none of the students understood the potential role of the tutor outside of academic issues.

Range of issues
The range of issues that students had felt it was appropriate to discuss with personal tutors was extensive. There were a considerable number of powerful stories of tutors impacting on often complex and entrenched social issues.

Case Study

From the very beginning of my course I really liked my personal tutor. I didn't see him often because everything had been going well but that changed during my second year. While I was home for the summer holidays my parents told me that they were separating. It was such a shock as I hadn't realised anything was wrong between them. Mum told me that Dad had been seeing someone else for a long time and that they had just tried to stay together until my younger sister and I had done our 'A' levels and left school. Dad left home immediately and moved in with his girlfriend. Mum struggled to get through each day and I felt like I had to look after both her and my sister, especially as my mum has multiple sclerosis. I felt as if my Dad had died, I couldn't believe that he had done this to us. We got by during the holidays but then it was time for me to go back to university. Part of me wanted to be able to leave and get away from everything, but I was worried about leaving them alone. For the first few months I tried to keep going and went home every weekend, but I think that there were just too many things to juggle. I wasn't getting the best out of being at university because I was never there at weekends to go out with everyone. I was getting behind with my work as I was also trying to work part-time in the evenings because money was an issue. I felt very alone and worried about how I would get through the rest of the year. After a lecture, given by my personal tutor, he stopped me as I was leaving and asked if everything was OK, as he had noticed that I was more subdued than usual. He sounded like he cared and I was so relieved to be able to talk to someone that I poured out everything that had been happening. I realised that there was nothing he could do to change things for me but it helped to have someone to listen to me. I felt that for the first time someone was putting my needs first. He arranged to see me each week to help me to plan a schedule to enable me to catch up with my work. He helped me to apply for extensions to assignments so that I had the holidays to try and catch up. I think that without his help and support I would have given up as everything seemed so difficult. I'm now at the end of my second year and things have got better. Mum is managing at home with the help of some family and friends and I do the best that I can in the holidays.

Of the students, 49 per cent had asked their personal tutors for support in dealing with stress and some students identified specific occasions when they had approached staff for support with periods of stress.

- I found it really hard to cope towards the end of last semester. Suddenly deadlines are looming and I can't imagine how I am going to get everything done. I've got a constant headache and I can't sleep. I went to see my personal tutor about something else and as she started to talk to me I started to cry.
- Stress is a major issue for me. I always seem to be juggling so much – being a mother, a wife, an employee and a student and most of it unsuccessfully!

Consistency

Many students expressed concern about what they perceived as a lack of consistency and/or knowledge on the part of staff.

- I get very confused by the different advice I get from personal tutors and module tutors.
- If I ask three different members of staff I get three completely different answers.

There was a need for students to operate in certainties rather than within a range of presented options. This led to an expectation that all staff would have a single perspective on all subjects. There appeared to be little understanding of the benefits and consequences of staff from different disciplines and backgrounds. A lack of consistency in approach by tutors was reported with regard to personal development planning (PDP). The value of PDP was of particular concern to mature students.

- My personal tutor has never mentioned PDP, but several of my friends' tutors make it part of every tutorial.
- My personal tutor told me that personal tutorials were entirely focused on the Student Qualities Profile (SQP). It took me a long time to work out what it actually was. I then didn't think that it was relevant to me as a mature student so I made no further attempts to contact my personal tutor and he has never contacted me. So I suppose it's not all that important really?

● Postgraduate experiences of personal tutors

We both have experience as postgraduate students. Alexa is currently studying an MA with the University of Exeter and Lindsey finished her MA at the University of Worcester in 2004. Our combined experiences led to the development of a series of questions which we presented to other postgraduate students from a variety of different higher education institutions. These case studies are presented as representative of the responses that we received.

Were you told who your personal tutor was?

Shahina   I was never allocated a named personal tutor. However, there was a lecturer who was responsible for postgraduate students and so whenever an issue arose that needed clarification or support I would contact him.

Laura   I wasn't officially told who my individual tutor was but there was one lecturer who managed the majority of my modules and so I contacted her for information and support.

David   Having attended postgraduate courses on a part-time basis at two universities I have had two different experiences. At the first I was not, to my knowledge, allocated a personal tutor. All enquiries were fed to the course leader. At the other I had a personal tutor named, but never had any contact from him. Fortunately, I did not require this type of support. However, each time I had an organisational query the only 'available' people were the department administration staff and the module leaders.

What kind of support did you receive from your named tutor, or in the absence of a named person, the tutor who appeared to assume the role?

Shahina   He always seemed interested in my progress and was quick to respond to queries, but there was always a feeling that time was too limited to explore any issues in depth.

Laura   She was able to answer most of my administration-based questions and she pursued any queries I had regarding course details by passing them on to the relevant lecturer.

David   The support was acceptable, but would have been improved if I had felt that there was a readily accessible point of contact to direct enquiries towards.

How different did you find the support you received as a postgraduate learner from that as an undergraduate learner?

Shahina   I think that there were few differences between the support I received but the main one was that as an undergraduate I had a named personal tutor.

Laura   Whilst during the first two years of my undergraduate study my personal tutor tended to get in contact with me to check on my welfare, both personal and work-related, whereas with my postgraduate study I find myself having to chase my personal tutor for simple admin/course details and this is all done via email.

David   As my postgraduate studies have all been on a part-time basis it was not as straightforward to obtain information and support as during my undergraduate studies. This did increase the level of stress and meant that there were conflicts between home, studies and work responsibilities.

How does this reflect what you understand of the differences between undergraduate and postgraduate study?

Shahina   As an undergraduate student, time is scheduled for you, you know what is expected of you in terms of what you will be doing and where you will be at any given time. As a postgraduate there is more freedom to prioritise and make personal decisions about patterns of working. This freedom brings with it an increased responsibility for recognising and acknowledging the pressures that exist. So, in some ways access to appropriate support is vital if post-graduate students are to cope with the additional pressures. I recognise that if difficult circumstances had arisen my studies would probably have had to be abandoned. A good relationship with a personal tutor would perhaps have enabled me to explore the stresses and find ways of restructuring the course commitments.

Laura   I understand it to mean that as a postgraduate student I have greater responsibility for managing my own time and that the course requires a greater amount of personal study and research without the reliance and regular support of tutors. I don't think that this should be reflected in the amount of available support from personal tutors.

David   While postgraduate studies are intended to be more student-driven, everyone can benefit from knowing that they can obtain support when they need it. I felt it was more a case of letting you get on with it and that there was little desire to be easily identified and contacted.

How do you think the support that you received affects the progress that you made on the course?

Shahina   I think that I probably completed the course because of my personal motivation to succeed. However, if that motivation had been compromised by other pressures then it would have taken a great deal of support and understanding to keep me on the course.

Laura   It has been beneficial simply to have an outlet for any concerns regarding the course itself and deadlines, which alleviates any study-related problems or worries, giving me more time to focus on the work itself.

David   On the whole it didn't affect my studies, but there were times when I would have appreciated the knowledge that somebody from the university was also considering my progress. It would have been beneficial to have had the real opportunity to talk through some of my options.

How important is the support of other learners?

Shahina   The support of other learners was not at all important to me but I was aware of others on the course who gained a great deal from peer support. In some ways it would have been a distraction for me. As an undergraduate this support was much more important.

Laura   As a distance learner I have not found the support of other learners to be particularly generally beneficia; however, the message-posting option on module websites worked well as a springboard for ideas and feedback.

David   I gained some benefit from linking up with some of the others who were on my modules, but as my postgraduate studies included two completely different groups it was difficult to get as much from it as I might have hoped.

During my undergraduate studies others were more helpful as we were all 'in the same boat' and studying full-time, so had similar needs.

If you experienced a personal problem during your studies, how would you hope that your personal tutor could help?

Shahina   I think that I would hope to have an opportunity to discuss my concerns with someone with whom I had already developed a relationship and who seemed interested and engaged and could offer the time that I needed.

Laura   By reassuring me and discussing the impact this problem would have on my work and perhaps pointing me in the direction of additional help if she was unable to help further.

David   While it would be helpful to have a tutor who was from the same discipline I think it is more useful to have somebody who is accessible and prepared to discuss concerns and, hopefully, be able to help resolve issues.

How important is electronic support for postgraduate students?

Shahina   Outside lectures most of my studies were undertaken in the late evening and at weekends, which is when I would have increased awareness of my support needs. Therefore I think that electronic support would have been the most appropriate for me, because requests for support, guidance and information can be made outside usual working hours.

Laura   I have had no contact with my personal tutor other than through email and so I would be lost without it. It also enables me to enquire about details/problems as I think of them and not simply within office hours. A form of instant contact such as messaging during office hours would have been useful on several occasions.

David   As my studies were on a part-time basis and my attendance at the university was concentrated into one or two days (generally afternoons and evenings) it was very important to be able to make contact through a variety of methods. Playing 'voicemail tennis' is never satisfactory and always frustrating. Using email means that a question can be posed and responded to at times which suit both the student and tutor.

What do you think the skills of a personal tutor are/should be?

Shahina   I think the skills of an effective personal tutor are basically those of a good communicator. They need to be both good listeners and approachable. The availability of protected time for personal tutorials is clearly an issue for staff but it is important to me that tutors are able to create the illusion of time by not answering the telephone or responding to callers at the door. Opportunities to build a relationship at the beginning of the course would encourage me to approach the tutor if need arises later in the course.

Laura   Firstly excellent communication skills are very important as this is the main way I 'use' my tutor, for communicating my own problems and also for her to relay information back to me. Accessibility and timing are also important as having a tutor who takes a long time to respond to queries is not only frustrating but can delay my progress on assignments.

David   The key to personal tutoring must be that they are comfortable with the role. From the student's perspective; the tutor needs to be identified early on, prepared to make themselves accessible and responsive, prepared to accept that they don't have the answer to every question, but will help to find another suitable person with the right skills and expertise.

These stories highlight a number of key issues that need to be taken into account when devising a personal tutoring system to meet the needs of postgraduate students. The personal tutor needs to be:

- named;
- identified at the beginning of the course;
- accessible;
- approachable;
- a good listener;
- equipped with referral skills.

These needs are little different from those of undergraduate students and so a model which meets the needs of undergraduate students is also likely to meet the needs of postgraduate students, although this will need to recognise the more flexible learning style of postgraduate study.

● The needs of distance learners

The code of practice for the assurance of academic quality and standards in higher education highlights the importance of personal tutoring for online and distance learners (QAA, 2004). The identification of a single contact is perhaps particularly important for the distance learners as they need to overcome a number of additional barriers to their learning.

Insights

As a distance learner I have found that there are difficulties that may affect both the quality of my work and the overall university experience. I consider these to be the lack of informal exchanges, networking, socialising and peer support. They can all assist with the motivation which is so essential to completing any long course of study. Being a distance learner also means that I don't have the opportunity to participate in university developmental activities such as the student council and student representatives' scheme. I have never been asked to take part electronically in a university-wide programme of this nature. I am also reliant upon my own personal IT skills and it can be frustrating not to have access to any technical support.

As an online and distance learner it is possible to feel emotionally as well as physically detached from the sources of support available to students following a more conventional route. The lack of possibilities for incidental meetings with either staff or other students can mean that difficulties are not resolved easily and informally. This may lead to an acceleration of difficulties and ultimately an abandonment of studies. Although many universities are now beginning to use text-based counselling this is unlikely to replicate the visible and accessible campus counselling services.

In addition to the isolation created by their chosen mode of learning, distance learners are also subject to the same pressures as those on a more conventional route. They may need more help with motivation because of the lack of opportunities for feedback and encouragement. There needs to be an emphasis on the response rates to students' emails as they are dependent on this form of communication. They do not have the same opportunity to access the student support services available to campus-based students. Whilst distance learners lack the benefits of face-to-face discussion and support, the increased level of communication via electronic sources does have advantages. Bolton (1999) highlights the value of writing out feelings and organising chaotic thoughts on paper.

Practical suggestions

☐ Promote university wide awareness of the potential pastoral needs of students.

☐ Ensure that all undergraduate, postgraduate and distance students have access to a designated personal tutor.

● Further reading

Bolton, G. (1999), *The Therapeutic Potential of Creative Writing: Writing Myself* (London: Jessica Kingsley).

Stanley, N. and Manthorpe, J. (2002), *Students' Mental Health Needs: Problems and Responses* (London: Jessica Kingsley).

Part Three

Student Support Services

5 Personal Tutoring and Student Services

Annie Grant

● The scope and organisation of student services

Within the higher education (HE) sector, the term 'student services' is commonly used to describe the range of information, advice and guidance offered to students centrally – that is, outside the academic department. Student services aim to promote students' wellbeing, primarily by helping them to overcome any practical or personal difficulties that might have a detrimental impact on their academic achievement. Many also offer opportunities for students to enhance their academic and personal skills, including those that will help them to make a successful transition to work or further study. Crucially, they offer a place to students to discuss issues and concerns in a confidential, neutral and non-judgemental environment with staff who are not involved in teaching them or assessing their work.

The last few decades have seen both an expansion and a diversification of student services in UK higher education institutions (HEIs), stimulated by, *inter alia*, the deterioration in staff–student ratios, the greater diversity of the student body as a result of widening participation initiatives, the increasingly complex legal and ethical framework in which HEIs now operate, and raised student expectations. These latter reflect not only the introduction of tuition fees but

---

This chapter explores the relationship between the departmentally based personal tutor and the advice and guidance services provided centrally for all students. The writer's aim is to provide information and guidance that will help tutors to be more effective in their role:

▶ briefly describing the additional support that may be available for the students centrally;
▶ giving guidance on referral and helping to clarify boundaries between the complementary roles of tutors and of student services personnel;
▶ suggesting some approaches to collaborative working to help resolve students' difficulties;
▶ outlining other ways in which student services professionals may be able to support academic staff in their role as personal tutors;
▶ offering some case studies to bring life to this discussion and exemplify some effective approaches and some where different tactics might have brought about a better outcome.

The chapter also provides a brief outline of some important issues for consideration by tutors, including confidentiality and record-keeping.

also societal changes that have made adults, and particularly young adults, less tolerant of poor provision than many of their predecessors.

Typically, HEIs offer specialist services and resources for students in many or all of the following areas:

- careers;
- counselling for students with significant personal and emotional difficulties;
- disability;
- learning support for students with specific learning difficulties, such as dyslexia and dyspraxia;
- mental and physical health;
- finance (administration of grants and loans, and money management);
- specialist advice for international students (including visa renewals, immigration, English language support and aculturalisation);
- academic writing and study skills;
- personal advice to help resolve practical difficulties, including legal problems;
- faith guidance and worship;
- wellbeing and good order in university accommodation;
- part-time work (for example through 'job shops');
- finding local accommodation and resolving problems with fellow students and neighbours;
- child care;
- fitness and sports coaching;
- and more.

In a number of institutions the student services also encompass some registry and administrative functions but these fall outside the main focus of this chapter.

There are many differences in the scale and scope of student service provision across the diverse HE sector. Some large institutions employ over 100 student services staff, many with very specific areas of professional expertise. In small institutions a few advisers may have to cover several different areas of expertise. In HEIs with limited institutional provision, student services staff may have to refer students to self-help resources or external providers within the local community. Even well resourced services form networks with other providers, including statutory bodies such as the NHS and local community and voluntary organisations.

The organisational structure of student services is also diverse. In some institutions a director of student services has overall responsibility for all provision and the focus is on addressing students' needs holistically. This approach may be reflected in the co-location of all functional areas, perhaps as a 'one-stop-shop'. In others, each functional area works semi-independently, but with a shared vision and a common set of policies and procedures. At the other extreme, student services may consist of a number of quite separate units, each with their own head, and with little or no cross-functional integration.

Student services vary not only in their organisational structure and in the scope of what they offer, but also in the ways they deliver their provision and in the models of advice, guidance and counselling that underpin their practice. This will be evident in most areas, but particularly in the counselling provision. Counsellors can have a wide range of therapeutic orientations and these inform the ways in which they work with their clients. Some services operate within a single orientation, while others employ more diverse approaches and, depending on the nature and context of the difficulties presented, may allocate students to counsellors working in particular ways.

The students' union can also play a role in the delivery of student services. Many unions provide general welfare advice and some offer student-run confidential night-time help lines, often branded as *Nightline*. The majority of students' unions offer advice and support for students who wish to take forward an academic appeal or complaint against their department or the institution; this is one of their most important advising functions. Their staff members are not on institutional payrolls and thus have a degree of independence that academic and student services staff cannot claim, however student-centred we may be. For further information about the scale, scope and organisation of student services in the UK see Grant (in press). One of the first tasks for any tutor should thus be to find out about:

- The range and scope of central provision in their own institution.
- Its organisational structure.
- The ways in which the services are provided (for example, through booked appointments, drop-in sessions, email and/or telephone enquiries, paper and web-based self-help resources; and/or central and departmentally-based workshops).
- The kind of support or guidance the student should expect to be offered.
- Where and when students can access the services.

If you have not already been given them, you should make sure that you have copies of any printed information leaflets outlining key services, and look at any web resources provided. A meeting with the head of student services might also be helpful, either individually or perhaps as a briefing session for all departmental tutors. It would be very surprising if your head of student services were to be other than delighted to offer this.

● Referral

If the tutorial system is working well, tutors will have established contact with their tutees at an early stage. Many students sail through university without any serious difficulties; their conversations with their tutors may stray little beyond academic issues and general matters. However, some students' queries, concerns or difficulties can move well beyond the academic sphere and other kinds of non-academic guidance or support may be requested. Alternatively, a tutor may suspect that a student is experiencing difficulties without their telling him or her, or may have heard of a student's difficulties from others.

Many tutors are both able and willing to offer personal advice or guidance themselves, and have the time and the skills to do so. However, even for committed tutors, there will be circumstances where they are not able, or it is not appropriate that they even try, to advise or guide the student themselves. One of the key roles for any personal tutor is thus that of referral. An effective personal tutor is able both to diagnose the nature of students' concerns or difficulties and also to determine who is best placed to provide the required information or offer suitable support. Even tutors who feel unsure about their ability to help students who present with serious personal concerns, or who do not feel that they have sufficient time to do so, fulfil a valuable role if they refer students to those with the appropriate specialist knowledge.

Many students find their way to the central services with little or no encouragement, but others, especially those who are feeling particularly distressed and at a loss, may find it difficult to approach those they have not met before and may need the encouragement of their tutor to do this. Exceptionally, it may be appropriate for you to make an appointment for a student, or let them use the phone in your office to do this. However, students are more likely to gain benefit from a referral if they have followed up your suggestion and taken the initiative themselves to book an appointment.

A common reason for student dissatisfaction is a mismatch between what a student is led to expect and what they are offered (see case study 5.1). It is

Case Study: Referral

In conversation with his tutor Angela, Trevor, a third year student, let slip that he was very worried about getting a job when he graduated; he was not at all sure what he wanted to do. He had made a few applications, but had not had a response from any of them. He wondered if Angela could look at his CV to see if that was the problem. Angela told him that she didn't really have any expertise in this area, but that he shouldn't worry; she was sure that the Careers Service would sort out his CV and tell him which would be the best kinds of jobs to apply for. She said that he should book himself in to see a careers adviser.

A week later, Trevor came to see Angela again to tell her that the Careers Service had not been at all helpful. They would not let him book an appointment until he had seen someone during one of their drop-in consultations, and they were already full for that day. They had given him a leaflet on writing CVs, and suggested that he try using a computer program to generate some career ideas. He hadn't found time to do this or read the booklet. He told Angela that he just wanted someone to tell him what to do.

Angela phoned the Careers Service to complain on Trevor's behalf. A careers adviser explained to her the reasons for the suggestions made to Trevor and that their aim was to help students to develop for themselves the skills and knowledge required to be successful both now and in the future. Their role was not to tell students what they should do. The resources he had been pointed to, including the diagnostic drop-in session, were offered in order to help him to take some initial steps for himself before he was booked in for a longer interview.

What worked well?
- Angela appropriately recognised that the Careers Service would be able to offer more comprehensive and up-to-date advice than she could.
- She followed up Trevor's complaint, and as a result of her better understanding of their approach and resources, was able to reassure Trevor that if he acted on the Careers Service's suggestion and did some initial preparatory work, he would be able to gain much more benefit from an interview with a careers adviser than if he went to the guidance interview unprepared.

Could the tutor have made the referral more effective?
Had Angela been clearer about what the Careers Service offered, and the guidance model that underpinned its provision, she might have been able to avoid Trevor's initial disillusion with the service.

very helpful if, when you refer students, you can outline accurately what the student can expect. If you are unsure about where best to refer a student, it is much better that you first ask for advice from someone within central services than that you refer inappropriately.

Referral should not be used as a means of avoiding difficult, awkward or confrontational situations, particularly when the tutor is in reality far better able to provide suitable information or guidance than anyone in student services. Just because a student bursts into tears, it does not mean that they need counselling or that there is a serious underlying problem. Your reassurance and the offer of a tissue or a glass of water may be all that is required; immediate referral to student services may be inappropriate. If you listen carefully to what a student is telling you, and ask appropriate open-ended questions, you should be able to determine who best can help.

When you have referred a student on, it is helpful if you follow up at your next meeting with the student. You might be able to provide additional guidance or support. At the very least, you will have demonstrated that you referred them on because you were genuinely concerned about them, and not because you wanted to get them out of your office.

● Role boundaries

Even for professionals, it can sometimes be difficult to know when to refer a student on to another colleague or an outside provider; it can be even more difficult if you begin to become personally involved with a student. This is perhaps more likely to happen within a departmental context, when a tutor may have known a student for several years.

It can also be very challenging for a tutor if a student shows reluctance to seek help elsewhere, or becomes over-dependent on them. A student may become angry and upset if a tutor, having offered apparently open-ended support, then backs away when the student demands more than the tutor can offer in terms of time, emotional commitment or professional skills. To prevent this happening, relationships between tutors and their tutees should always remain on a professional footing. Tutors can and should be friendly to their tutees, but they should not try to be their friends, or indeed their surrogate parents. It is rarely, if ever, appropriate for tutors to give students their home contact details or mobile phone numbers, even when there is concern about the possibility of an impending crisis. If you contact student services they will give you the appropriate numbers to pass on to a student; these may include a 24-hour institutional contact number (usually the internal security service), external numbers such as the emergency services or NHS Direct, and the relevant internal student service office hours number.

Tutors should clarify from the outset with their tutees where the boundaries in their relationship lie, what a student can expect of them, and in what circumstances they would support a student by referring them to another provider. They may also need to be clear that even if a student is unwilling to seek help elsewhere, there may be situations where the tutor would not feel able or appropriately trained to act or give guidance. Many institutions have produced information for tutors on what is expected of them, and where boundaries for their role might reasonably lie. Student services staff will usually also be happy to discuss boundary issues with you. Case study 5.2 explores some of the issues raised above in more detail.

Conflicts of interest

Tutors should be aware of the potential for conflicts of interest in circumstances where they also teach and assess the work of their tutees. This can be particularly sensitive when students are on a professional course and tutors are concerned that the difficulties the students wish to talk about may have 'fitness to practice' implications.

In the early tutorial systems established in Oxford and Cambridge colleges, the 'moral tutor' provided personal support while academic guidance was provided by a director of studies. This separation was maintained in many tutorial systems in other institutions, but in recent years it has become common for tutors to provide both academic guidance and personal support. This in part reflects declining staff – student ratios, but also recognises that students' academic and personal concerns are frequently closely bound together, and that a 'holistic' perspective can be very valuable for the student. However, if either a student or a tutor feels that in the resolution of a particular set of circumstances conflicting interests may present themselves, referral to student services might offer a solution.

● Working with student services

It may be entirely appropriate to refer a student on to one of the central student services for help. However, there are not infrequently situations where a joint or collaborative approach offers the best way forward for both the student and the tutor, as long as the student is willing for some information to be shared.

Sometimes referral is in the opposite direction. Many of the students who consult student services have made direct contact without being referred by

---

Case Study: Boundaries

A tutor, Janet, had significant experience of tutoring and had just become the department's senior tutor. She enjoyed the role, and wanted to set a good example for all the other tutors in her department. For some months she had been seeing a tutee, Max, on a fairly regular basis. He often called in to see her, and she was enjoying the feeling of being able to help him stay the course. His health difficulties had been affecting his academic work and Janet had negotiated extensions to academic deadlines; he was managing to get his work in. However, his marks still didn't reflect what she and Max considered to be his real potential. Max had also often seemed rather low, but Janet put this down to his physical health. She told him that he could come to see her whenever he was feeling down.

Late one Friday afternoon, just as Janet was about to leave to pick up her son from the nursery, Max appeared in her office looking much more distressed than ever before. He had heard yesterday that he had failed a course assessment, and hadn't slept since as he was so worried about it. He told her that he once took an overdose in the past and was frightened that he might do it again. Janet briefly tried to reassure him, but said that she couldn't stay to talk to him as she was in a hurry. She suggested that he go back to his university room to get some rest, and perhaps find a friend to be with him. She said that she would phone him later and checked his mobile number. It was now after 5 p.m., but on her way to pick up her child, she phoned student services in a panic to ask them to try to ensure that the student was alright as she was going away for the weekend. Fortunately, there was still someone experienced in the office.

---

departmental staff. Sometimes this is because a student does not wish the department to know about their personal difficulties, or even because the perceived cause of their difficulties lies within their department. While it is often possible for student services to help students to find a way forward, to resolve their queries or difficulties without contacting the department, there are often situations where they can only provide a partial solution on their own.

For example, if the student's difficulties are having an impact on his or her ability to sustain academic work, the personal tutor may be able to help the student to prioritise coursework tasks, negotiate extensions to deadlines, and provide notes for missed classes. At the same time student services might be able to work with the student to help find a solution to their more personal difficulties (see case study 5.3).

What worked well?
- The tutor demonstrated her interest in the student, and made him feel comfortable and able to seek her help.
- The tutor negotiated appropriate extended coursework deadlines for the student, and this helped him to complete his academic work despite his ill health.

Could the tutor have responded differently?
- The tutor almost certainly 'held on' to the student too long. Had she encouraged him to seek additional advice and support from the student services, his underlying depression might have been picked up sooner. His crisis might have been averted, or he would at least have been known to student services staff, who would have been in a better position to help when the crisis came.
- The student services staff member who responded to her call was placed in an extremely difficult position. He was being asked by Janet to respond in a very sensitive situation to a student he did not know, and about whom he had no substantive background information.
- The student might have benefited early on from contact with a number of different student services. These could have included the counselling service, the mental health service, and perhaps even the academic learning service, where he might have been helped to find more effective ways of prioritising his work and planning his time.

It is often possible for student services to work collaboratively with a tutor without divulging the full details of the student's problems to the tutor. It may be enough to know from student services that the difficulties that the student is facing are significant enough to warrant academic concessions being made. Each institution will have its own regulations in respect of the evidence required to support such concessions, but these should provide the flexibility to allow the student to maintain some level of confidentiality as long as there is a report from a professional that records their judgement of the severity of the difficulties, and the likely impact these will have on the student's ability to study. Confidentiality and record keeping are further explored below.

Case study 5.3 raises another issue. Sometimes a student's difficulties can have a significant impact on his or her friends. Students are frequently

Case Study: Working in partnership

Alex first came to the attention of Simon, a senior member of student services staff, when several anxious students asked to talk urgently to him. They reported that Alex was acting very strangely in seminars. He was dominating all discussions with loud interventions which mainly consisted of streams of consciousness or insistence on reading long passages of text out loud. His fellow students were both worried about his state of mind and concerned about the impact of his behaviour on their own learning. They had tried to get him to seek help as they knew that he had had difficulties in the past, but he resolutely refused. They were also cross that the seminar teacher was not taking any action, and leaving the students to cope with the disturbances caused by Alex. The students did not feel able to raise the matter in the department themselves as they did not want Alex to know that they had talked to anyone else about him; they were also reluctant to criticise the seminar teacher.

The immediate priority for Simon was to attend to the students who had come to seek help and reassurance and advice was offered to them. Simon's next step was to talk to Nadia, Alex's tutor, outlining the key issues without revealing the source of his information. Nadia spoke to the seminar teacher and pointed out to him that it was his responsibility to ensure that seminars were not disrupted, even if that meant asking Alex to leave.

Simon and Nadia agreed to meet Alex together to encourage him to seek professional support. After some persuasion Alex agreed to come to the meeting. While at first he showed no insight into his situation, he finally agreed to seek help and ultimately withdrew from his course temporarily.

What worked well?
- By contacting the tutor, student services were able to ensure that there was no further disruption to fellow students in the seminar class.
- In presenting a sympathetic but clear, firm and united approach to Alex, Simon and Nadia were able together to persuade Alex to withdraw from the course and seek professional help. Then, once he had begun to improve, they were able together to help him continue his studies: student services provided personal support, and his tutor academic guidance.

What more might have been done?
- In this case, it was clear in retrospect that had action been taken earlier, less disruption might have been caused to fellow students and Alex might also have been persuaded to seek help sooner. The seminar teacher had lacked either the confidence or the requisite skills to approach Alex about his behaviour early on.

extremely loyal to their friends and reluctant to break confidences. However, they may be carrying a significant burden, particularly if the student in question is seriously ill, self-harming or threatening suicide. As a tutor you may be in a position to speak to a student's friendship group directly and remind them of the relevant student services should they feel they need to seek help for themselves.

Responding to a diverse student body

The demographics of the student body have changed significantly as Britain's higher education system has moved from one that aimed to recruit an intellectual (and frequently, consequently social) elite, to one that aims to include all those who have the ability and motivation to gain benefit from the opportunities offered. Tutors are often faced with queries or situations for which their own knowledge or life experiences have not equipped them to respond. Collaboration with, or advice from, student services can help them to manage unfamiliar situations and reduce some of the pressures and anxieties that can be inherent in their role. This section briefly draws attention to just some of the areas and issues that tutors may find particularly demanding or unfamiliar.

Students with disabilities and specific learning difficulties

One of the significant successes of widening participation initiatives is that many students who would previously have been denied the opportunity of higher education because of a disability or specific learning difficulty are successfully completing degree courses. Supporting and advising such students often requires a level of specialist knowledge or experience that tutors are unlikely to have themselves. Most students who have declared a disability are known to the disability staff in student services and many are in regular contact for specialist academic learning support or advice on, or help with, necessary practical arrangements. A key role for the tutor can be as the link between student services and the department on behalf of the student. Specialist staff can advise the tutor about the adjustments or additional facilities required for their tutee; these may be advance lecture notes, presentations in a large font, hearing loops in seminar rooms, consideration of the impact of dyslexia when marking written work, and so on. The tutor can ensure that relevant information is passed on to other teaching and administrative staff so that any necessary adjustments are made.

Some institutions have taken the step of setting up a network of 'disability liaison' staff within departments. These act as a point of contact between central disability specialists and academics. Such systems work best when the departmental representatives take on the role with enthusiasm, are willing to keep in close contact with the disability office and take advantage of any training offered, and play an active role in disseminating knowledge and understanding to colleagues. However, there can be a downside, particularly when the role is undertaken by those who are not really committed to the task, or when the presence of a disability 'specialist' within the department is used as an excuse by others for not engaging fully with the issues.

Students with serious personal and mental health difficulties

There is growing evidence of a rise in the proportion of students who are experiencing serious personal or psychological difficulties that threaten to impede their ability to function academically. Tutors may be the first to notice that a student's mental health is deteriorating. They may notice changes in the student's behaviour or appearance, or have picked up the concerns from other colleagues, including reports of absence from lectures and classes. It can be very challenging for any tutor to know how to respond to such students; early contact with student services (usually the mental health co-ordinator or the counselling service) to seek their advice is likely to be beneficial for both the tutor and the student. You will find more detailed guidance on responding to a student with mental health difficulties on the University of Lancaster's (2002) web resource; there is also useful background information in Stanley and Manthorpe's (2002) book on student mental health.

Under 18-year-olds

Many institutions routinely admit at least a small number of students each year who are under 18 years old. There may be more such students admitted in future now that the recently introduced age discrimination legislation makes it unlawful to deny admittance to a student simply on the grounds of age. Students under 18 are minors in the eyes of the law, and universities have an implied enhanced duty of care towards them until the date at which they attain their majority. Your own institution is almost certain to have developed a policy and procedures to ensure that this duty is fulfilled and you should make yourself aware of any implications these have for you as a tutor. You might, for example, be required to have a Criminal Records Bureau (CRB) check, or to see your under-18-year-old tutees more frequently than other students. Student services once again may be able to guide or support you.

Gender

For some students it is, or becomes, important to them to have a tutor of their own sex. If a tutee asks to change to a different tutor, it is helpful if you make this as easy as possible, without asking for a detailed explanation. If this is not possible, then a suggestion that the student is referred to someone in student services for personal guidance might offer an alternative solution.

Students from diverse ethnic, cultural and religious backgrounds

Knowing how to respond appropriately to a student from an unfamiliar cultural or ethnic background can be very challenging. International students in particular may react to situations or advice in ways that are not those that you predict and may be unfamiliar with the network of support offered by student services. For example, in some cultures there is a stigma attached to

---

Case Study: Religious diversity

Mohammed, came to see his adviser, Sally, as he had just found out that one of his core seminars clashed with Friday prayers; as a devote Muslim he was very concerned. He wanted to know if Sally could arrange for the lecture slot to be changed, or could give him permission to miss the class and make up the work afterwards from course notes. Sally did not know at first how to respond. Her initial reaction was one of slight irritation. One part of her wanted to be sympathetic, but on the other hand she felt that if she were to make an exception for Mohammed, other students might feel that they had other good reasons for missing seminars and want similar dispensations. She was not really sure of the status of Friday prayers, and wondered if Mohammed couldn't go to the Mosque to pray on other days or at other times.

However, she hid her irritation and decided not to give an immediate response. She told Mohammed that she would make some enquiries and email him shortly. She then contacted Alice in student services to ask what she should do.

Alice, in consultation with the Muslim Chaplain, was first able to clarify the requirements for Muslims in relation to Friday prayer. She suggested that Mohammed should talk to the Muslim Chaplain, and that together with Sally, they find a way forward for the coming semester. Alice told Sally that she had had a number of similar enquiries and she would be working on the development of a cross-institutional policy on religious observance.

What worked well?

- By resisting her first instinct to dismiss Mohammed's request and seeking advice, the tutor was able to clarify her understanding of the situation and, in collaboration with others, find a compromise solution. Involving student services helped alert them to an issue whose resolution was best addressed at an institutional level.

those referred for counselling. If a student is reluctant to seek help from one service, even if it seems to you to be the most appropriate place for them, but has already established a good relationship with another, then this latter might provide the most appropriate initial referral point. Student services' international student advisers have usually made contact with all international students at an early stage, and may therefore be the best initial referral point for the student, and a source of guidance for you.

Despite the secularisation of UK society, in many ways we still operate within a broadly Christian paradigm; this can create practical as well as adjustment difficulties for students from other faiths. Many institutions have multi-faith chaplaincies and can provide guidance for tutors on faith matters. Case study 4 explores one such issue in more detail.

● Enhancing learning, personal and professional skills

The discussion so far has focused on some of the difficulties that students face. However, the roles of both tutor and student services staff are by no means restricted to problem solving: both can offer guidance that can help students to raise their academic performance, and prepare for a successful transition to employment or further study.

An increasing number of institutions now include an academic learning or skills development unit within their student services. These units offer opportunities for students to seek impartial guidance on generic academic matters. One of their aims is to help students who are at risk of failing, or whose prior educational experience has not prepared them well for the kinds of study and assessment tasks required for higher education. Such units often also work with those who are doing well but want to further improve their grades or seek guidance on a particular topic of concern. You may thus be able to recommend your institution's provision to all students who you feel are not achieving their full academic potential. If you make this referral a very positive one, you can avoid students who are concerned about failure feeling stigmatised.

Students choose to come to university for a wide variety of reasons, but for the majority, the expectation that the possession of a degree will advance their career prospects is a key factor. Institutions and individual departments are also increasingly judged by the early career success of their students through the inclusion of so called 'employability' measures in league tables. One sector-wide approach to helping students to develop their skills has been the requirement by the Higher Education Funding Council for England (HEFCE) for institutions to offer their students a personal development planning programme that encourages self-reflection and personal development. In some HEIs, tutors are explicitly involved in the implementation of this programme.

Professional information and guidance in this area is often the remit of the institutional careers service, but there is a key role for the tutor to play in encouraging students to think about preparing for their next steps at an early stage and in outlining the services and opportunities offered by the careers service. A tutor can also encourage students to become involved in those extra-curricular activities that offer them opportunities to develop and extend their skills and experience; the careers centre will usually be able to suggest the means once the tutor has stimulated the student's interest.

● Support for advisers

The role of personal tutor can be very challenging, particularly when the tutees present with complex or very serious difficulties. Many institutions' staff development units organise structured training for tutors, often delivered by staff from student services; such training can be particularly valuable for staff new to the role. Additionally, advice and support on an ongoing basis is often also available from student services staff, who are usually more than willing to act as 'consultants' to tutors concerned about how to respond to a student. Such indirect student guidance via the tutor can be as effective for a student as a direct referral, particularly when a trusting relationship between tutor and tutee has been established. The guidance from student services can also help tutors to feel more confident and effective in their role, less stressed, and more able to refer their tutees on to student services at the appropriate time.

When a tutor has been involved in a particularly difficult or emotionally challenging situation, for example a student death or a serious breakdown, debriefing by student services staff may be very helpful. Most student counselling services, even if they do not officially provide counselling for staff, will offer time to a tutor who is trying to resolve anxieties that relate to their work with students. Student services may be very willing to arrange a debriefing session for all those involved in a crisis situation or a student death.

Many student services have developed web and paper-based resources specifically for tutors. Some institutions provide detailed manuals for their tutors; others offer more specific guidance, particularly on mental health and disability issues. If your institution has not yet produced its own materials, it is worth undertaking a web search as many resources for personal tutors have been posted on institutional websites. A recent book (Thomas and Hixenbaugh, 2006) explores personal tutoring in several UK institutions.

● Confidentiality

In establishing the boundaries in your relationship with your tutees, and in working with others, including student services, the issue of confidentiality will inevitably arise. Doctors, clergy and counsellors are bound by strict professional and ethical guidelines and will rarely, if ever, reveal any personal information about those who have consulted them. However, the limits of confidentiality can be less clear cut in respect of internal communication within a personal-tutor or a general student-services context.

Students should be helped to feel that they can trust their tutors so that they are able to talk freely to them, but tutors and other staff do not necessarily have a duty to maintain strict confidentiality within the department or institution. It is, however, very important that tutors treat personal information about a student with discretion, and only pass on that information to colleagues when there is good reason to do so. If you are concerned about how to respond to a student you may be able to discuss your concerns in general terms without naming the student. On the other hand, if you are concerned that a student might be in difficulties, either through your own conversations with him or her, or as a result of remarks made by others, sharing your concerns with colleagues may help you to gain a better understanding of the extent and impact of the student's difficulties and decide on an appropriate course of action.

The issue of confidentiality is clearer when it comes to communication with those outside the institution. Tutors and student services personnel are frequently contacted by concerned relatives or friends asking for information. You may be a parent yourself and feel sympathy with the enquirer and wish to help, or the enquirer may become assertive or even aggressive. Parents may argue that they are paying the student's fees and therefore they have a right to know. However, unless you have the explicit permission of the student, it is very rarely appropriate, or even legal, to pass on any personal information about another individual.

This is not to say that you should refuse to talk to the enquirer. It might be helpful to outline the provision available for all students at your institution. For example, if the enquirer is worried about a student being homesick, or being ill and missing a deadline, you can talk in general terms about the range of social activities available on campus, or the systems that the university has for granting deadline extensions or taking mitigating circumstances into account when marking work. If the enquirer is concerned about not having heard from the student, you can offer to encourage the student to make contact, or to forward a letter, but the rider to any such offer should be 'if I find that they are a student at this university'. This may seem to be an over-cautious approach, but some students, in order to ensure their own safety and wellbeing, may need to keep their presence at university a secret from others; these latter may include parents or those who identify themselves as friends or other family members. All students, even those who are under 18, have a right to have their privacy respected. Confidentiality must of course be broken when there is clear risk of harm to self or others, or when required by law.

● Record-keeping

Good record-keeping is crucial. Tutors may wish to keep their own notes on their tutees but it is good practice to have a departmental filing system where both routine and more personal records on each student are kept. Sometimes the seriousness of a student's difficulties only becomes apparent when the views or experiences of a number of staff are brought together. All records should be kept in a secure place, with access limited to a defined group of staff: those who need to know for administrative and academic purposes or to ensure the wellbeing of the student. It is good practice to ask a student if they are happy for you to keep notes of your meetings. If a student is initially concerned about this, you may be able to gain their agreement by showing your notes to them at the end of each meeting. Students have the right to insist that they do not wish you to pass on any personal information about them to anyone else, including others in your department. If they do this, you may need to explain that this could limit your ability to provide evidence in the future if they wish to apply for concessions, or to provide the student with the best possible support or guidance.

File notes on students should consist of clear and concise factual information. When it is necessary to record an opinion, for example to record a tutor's growing concerns about a student in the absence of any factual information at that point, then the notes should make clear that what is written is opinion and not fact. Judgemental views on a student should be avoided: the personal view of one member of staff should not be allowed to cloud or influence the views or judgements of others. Those writing and compiling records should also be aware of the implications of the legislation concerning data protection and freedom of information. For example, the current data protection legislation gives students the right to see the content of any files held on them. The website of the Information Commissioner's Office (www.ico.gov.uk/) is a very useful and clear resource for any tutor who wishes to understand more about the law on data protection and the rights, responsibilities and obligations of the 'data subjects' and those who hold the data.

● Summary

In an increasingly impersonal HE environment, tutors play a very important role in helping to personalise the learning experience for students, and in so doing support both their academic learning and their overall development. However, most tutors are themselves under pressure and may feel ill-equipped to respond to some of the difficulties that students bring to them. This chapter has aimed to help tutors to use their time and contribution to student wellbeing more effectively through relevant referral to, and collaborative working with, their institutional student services.

An initial investment of time in gaining a broad knowledge of the range of student services available locally and the ways in which they operate is likely to offer benefits to both tutors and tutees. Student services staff are usually not only willing to advise or guide tutors who wish to know how best to respond to their tutees, but also to offer more personal support to tutors who become anxious or concerned themselves as a result of their work in response to student difficulties and crises.

Tutors have the advantage of both formal and informal interaction with students in the 'normal' day-to-day environment; many student services staff only see students who are experiencing difficulties. An ongoing relationship between tutors and student services can help the latter to gain a better and broader understanding of the student experience and make it easier for them to be pro-active in developing their own, and when relevant, institutional provision and policies to meet changing circumstances and student expectations.

Practical suggestions

☐ Invest time in finding out about the range of student services and resources offered in your institution. This will help you to refer students to the appropriate specialist staff when they present with difficulties that you are not able, or do not have the time, to resolve.

☐ When you refer a student to another source of information or advice, follow up afterwards. This helps the student know that your referral does not mean that you are no longer interested in advising them. It may be appropriate to make it clear that you are happy to help them to manage their course work, but that it is best for the student if they consult student services staff in respect of any personal or heath difficulties.

☐ Some students will come from backgrounds or hold beliefs that are unfamiliar to you, or may react to situations in ways that surprise you. Establishing a trusting and effective relationship will be easier if you show that you are open and willing to listen, and can avoid making judgements.

☐ Make sure that you are familiar with all the relevant university policies, procedures and practices, for example, those concerning students who are under 18, students with disabilities or mental health difficulties, fitness to practice, and student discipline.

☐ Establish a professional relationship with a key member or members of your student services department who can give you advice when you are unsure how to respond to a student, or support when you are facing a particularly challenging situation.

☐ Keep your relationships with students on a professional footing and avoid getting too personally involved in their difficulties. Knowing when and to whom to refer a student is crucial for students' and your own wellbeing.

☐ If you suspect that a student is experiencing difficulties, try to find an opportunity to talk to them at an early stage so that you help to minimise any impact on their academic studies. Don't forget too that a student's difficulties may also be having a detrimental impact on their friends or classmates.

> ☐ Students, of course, have a right to privacy and it is there-
> fore important to try as much as possible not to identify
> them individually if you need to discuss their personal
> concerns with others. Be particularly careful about giving
> any information about a student to anyone outside the
> university, including those who identify themselves as
> parents, unless you have the student's express permission.

> ☐ Make clear, factual and non-judgemental notes of your
> interactions with students and make sure that they are
> filed in a central departmental filing system to which
> access is strictly limited.

> ☐ Don't forget that an ongoing relationship between advisers
> and student services staff can help the latter to improve
> their understanding of the academic and personal chal-
> lenges faced by students and advisers, and thus develop
> their provision and resources in response.

● Further reading

Grant, A. (in press), 'Student Services in the United Kingdom – an Overview', in
    K. J. Osfield and Associates (eds), *The Internationalization of Student Affairs
    and Services in Higher Education: An Emerging Global Perspective*
    (Washington: NASPA).
Stanley, N. and Manthorpe, J. (eds) (2002), *Students' Mental Health Needs:
    Problems and Responses* (London: Jessica Kingsley).
Thomas, L. and Hixenbaugh, P. (eds) (2006), *Personal Tutoring in Higher
    Education* (Stoke on Trent: Trentham Books).
University of Lancaster (2002), *Student Mental Health Planning, Guidance and
    Training Manual*, www.studentmentalhealth.org.uk/ (accessed 1 November
    2006).

6 Supporting Equality and Diversity

Rebecca Harrison

This chapter will explore the legislative framework which guides institutional approaches to equality and diversity, and which has undergone significant change in the last seven years. Government-led initiatives to increase inclusion in higher education over the same period have also resulted in greater student diversity. It will provide the working knowledge of equality legislation that personal tutors today require, to be effective in this environment. It will also help develop the understanding and skills necessary to appropriately support students who are different from the personal tutor and each other.

● Introduction

Long gone are the days when higher education was the preserve of wealthy young men, when both students and lecturers came from the same educational background and social class. It was then relatively easy for academic staff to support students' learning and assist them with any problems. Those few students from outside this community, those with different learning styles, from overseas or from a poorer background, were required to adapt to the teaching and support available or risk failure. Today universities strive to support the learning of a very diverse student population. As a result, personal tutors are in contact with a variety of students, including many students with whom they may have very little in common. It is now up to the academic staff to adapt, for it is they who are expected to develop new strategies and tools for supporting the learning of students who are different from themselves.

The diversity of students in higher education has many aspects – ethnicity, nationality, disability, gender, sexual orientation, religion, family structure, socio-economic group, age, educational background, mode of study . . . the list is almost endless. Further, students do not fall neatly into one category or another, they usually sit across several. This can mean that students are as different from each other as they are from their tutors. There is, therefore, a need for all university staff to develop an understanding of diversity in its broadest sense and the issues it raises.

Tutors within higher education also need to be aware of the political nature of diversity today. The government has launched several initiatives over the last five years to increase participation in higher education, particularly amongst ethnic and socio-economic groups traditionally under-represented. There has also been a suite of equality legislation that has come into force. Since 2000, new legislation addressing disability, race, religion and gender has been enacted. Whilst the main focus of much of this legislation is in the area of employment, some is specifically aimed at addressing issues of institutionalised discrimination and therefore has a direct impact on higher education policy and practice.

● Legislative framework

In the last six years the government has enacted several pieces of legislation aimed at addressing issues of equality and diversity. Some of this legislation has been very prescriptive as to the actions public bodies, such as higher education institutions, must undertake. This legislation includes the Race Relations (Amendment) Act 2000, the Equality Bill (2005) and the Disability Discrimination Act (1995 and 2005). Other recent legislation extends or clarifies legal protection against discrimination to particular groups, this legislation includes: the Racial and Religious Hatred Bill 2005, the Employment Equality (Sexual Orientation) Regulations 2004 and the Employment Equality (Age) Regulations 2006. However, these latter pieces of legislation do not require institutions to take any positive action, only to refrain from discriminatory practices. Some institutions have nevertheless used this legislation as an opportunity to review policy and/or take forward initiatives to improve equality.

As the Race Relations (Amendment) Act, Equality Bill and Disability Discrimination Act are specifically targeted at public bodies such as universities they require some detailed explanation. The Race Relations Act and Equality Bill are discussed further here and the Disability Discrimination Act is covered in more detail in Chapters 5 and 10.

Race Relations (Amendment) Act (2000)

The Race Relations (Amendment) Act 2000, called the RRAA, was part of the government's response to the Macpherson Report on the inquiry into the murder of the young black man Stephen Lawrence. The RRAA requires public bodies to take active steps to eliminate discrimination and to promote equality and good relations between the races. In order to ensure compliance, institutions were required to publish a Race Equality Action Plan which details the activities and actions they would undertake to fulfil the requirements of the legislation. The Commission for Racial Equality has been given oversight of all public sector action plans and the power to reject plans that are, in their opinion, not sufficiently robust. Under the RRAA, universities are required to monitor the admission and progression of students and the recruitment of staff by racial group and, where there is evidence of particular racial groups being disadvantaged, action must be taken to identify the cause and address the problem. All public bodies are also required to undertake impact assessments of all their policies and procedures to ensure that they are not affecting racial groups differently. Impact assessments require both the analysis of institutional policies and procedures as well as consultation with staff, students and the wider community. This consultation is intended to enable groups to give feedback on the effects of institutional processes as well as providing a collaborative approach to resolving areas of concern.

Equality Bill 2005

The Equality Bill 2005 provides additional protection from discrimination based on religion, belief or gender. The Equality Bill, much like the RRAA, requires public bodies to prepare a Gender Equality Plan, which is to detail the actions institutions are taking to ensure gender equality. Institutions must also monitor staff and students by gender to ensure equality and must conduct impact assessments of policies and procedures in the same manner as with the RRAA.

The Equality Bill also changes the way in which equality issues will be overseen within the UK. The Bill created the Commission for Equality and Human Rights (CEHR), which, as the name implies, will have a broad remit to oversee equality issues. The CEHR will initially join the Equal Opportunities Commission and the Disability Rights Commission into a single entity, and also subsume the Commission for Racial Equality in 2009. The Commission for Equality and Human Rights will have oversight of compliance with all of the equality legislation listed above and it is with this commission that universities will continue to communicate about compliance with equality legislation.

● Responding to legislation

What does this legislation mean to personal tutors?

It is important for all academic staff to understand what constitutes discrimination as institutions can be prosecuted if any of their activities are found to be discriminatory. It should also be noted that where a staff member acts in a way that is overtly discriminatory, they may face individual legal action as well as internal disciplinary proceedings.

In order to avoid difficulties it is important for personal tutors to be completely clear about what constitutes discrimination. Discrimination quite often is thought of as actions such as using derogatory names. This form of discrimination is referred to as harassment and most universities will have policies and procedures to address it. The *A-Z of Equality and Diversity* (AUA et al., 2005, p. 21) gives the following definition of harassment:

> Harassment is unwanted conduct which may create the effect of violating a person's dignity or creating an intimidating, hostile, degrading, humiliating or offensive environment or induces stress, anxiety, fear or sickness on the part of the harassed person. The defining features are that the behaviour appears or feels offensive, humiliating, hostile or intimidating to the recipient or would be so regarded by a reasonable person.   (p. 21)

However, discrimination goes beyond harassment. It includes any action or inaction which disadvantages particular groups or individuals for reason of their membership of a particular group. Once again the the *A-Z of Equality and Diversity* (AUA et al., 2005, p. 11) offers a useful definition. It defines discrimination as follows:

> Discrimination takes place when an individual or group of people is treated less favourably than others because of factors unrelated to their merit, ability or potential. It is unlawful to discriminate against someone on grounds of their sex (including gender reassignment), sexual orientation, marital status, race, colour, nationality, ethnic origin, religion, beliefs, disability . . .   (p. 11)

A personal tutor, therefore, must ensure that they treat all students with respect and avoid any behaviour which might reasonably cause a student embarrassment or distress as defined by the legislation. Any concern raised by a student about behaviour, yours or others', that is causing them to feel uncomfortable must be taken seriously. The failure to respond to concerns raised by a student about discrimination or harassment can be considered discriminatory and illegal in its own right.

All universities will have policies on discrimination and harassment and should have formal mechanisms whereby students or staff can report concerns or specific incidences for redress. It is important for personal tutors to be aware of these procedures within their own institution, so that they are able to confidently guide students to these systems if required. It can be vital for a student who is experiencing discrimination to feel that they have support from the university. Their personal tutor can play an important role creating this feeling of support by listening sympathetically to their concerns and offering informed advice about the alternatives open to them in dealing with the situation.

In addition to specific policies on harassment and discrimination, universities will also have published race, disability and gender action plans in order to ensure full compliance with the legislation. All public bodies have a duty to promote equality of opportunity and take steps to prevent discrimination for reasons of race, gender or disability. The Race Equality Action Plans, Disability Equality Schemes and Gender Equality Plans lay out the steps the university will be taking to promote equality and prevent discrimination. It is advisable for tutors to be aware of the details of their own university's plan and in particular of any training or activities prescribed for staff in these documents.

Although not considered to be equality legislation, and currently only applicable in England, the Higher Education Act 2004, which enabled the introduction of top-up tuition fees and established the Office for Fair Access (OFFA) should be mentioned. Under the conditions of the Higher Education Act, top-up fees could only be charged by institutions which committed to increasing the participation of students from groups traditionally under-represented in higher education. Institutions which chose to charge top-up fees were required to submit to OFFA an access agreement detailing the measures which the institution would undertake in order to support students from non-traditional backgrounds, including the provision of financial support. As with institutional action plans, personal tutors would find it useful to be aware of their own universities' OFFA Access Agreements as these may detail specific support which will be made available to some groups of students.

Finally, personal tutors should be aware of the growing government concern about radical Islamic groups and their alleged recruitment activities on university campuses. In November 2006 the Department for Education and Skills (DfES) issued guidance to universities about monitoring the activities of Islamic groups on campus (DfES, 2006). This guidance recommends that institutions proactively monitor the activities of student groups and the external speakers invited onto the campus. This action by the government has been controversial and many within the sector have expressed concerns about Islamic students being singled out for monitoring, and universities being asked to serve as watchdogs (Universities UK, November 2006). It is too early to assess what, if any, impact this guidance may have on the relationship between Islamic students and their universities. However, tutors will need to be sensitive to the possibility that some students may be aware of this guidance and feel less open or trusting of university staff as a consequence.

An understanding of the legislation and government guidance related to equality is only a small part of the knowledge and skills which a personal tutor needs, to work effectively with student diversity. There are also personal skills that can be developed which can help them to work and communicate effectively with students from a variety of backgrounds.

● Multi-cultural issues

Often, when thinking about diversity, the first association is one of ethnicity or country of origin. This is, of course, one part of the diversity in higher education. HESA statistics for 2004/05 show 318,395 international students and 121,265 home students from ethnic minority groups studying in higher education. However, student diversity is much broader than this. Personal tutors today are increasingly required to be sensitive to diversity in its broadest sense. Reflecting legislation, universities are becoming more aware of issues related to disability, race and gender. Widening participation initiatives have increased the numbers of students entering higher education through non-traditional routes or from groups that traditionally have been under-represented. Students included within this widening participation agenda include mature students, those without traditional pre-entry qualification and those from areas where higher education attainment is very low.

The ever-increasing diversity of students means that, to be effective, personal tutors need to move beyond compartmentalising students into a particular type, e.g. far eastern, black, gay, and utilising set responses based on group assignation. Rather, tutors should begin to consider diversity in terms of any difference from themselves. The skills required to work effectively with difference have been identified and discussed within the literature in a number of professional areas relevant to personal tutors, teaching (Prosser, 2001), counselling (Corey, 1991) and student services work (Winston et al., 2001).

The counselling and student service literature in particular have proposed models of multi-cultural competence for one-to-one working with individuals which should prove useful to personal tutors. It is suggested that the starting point for multi-cultural competency is an examination and understanding of one's own beliefs and attitudes. For a personal tutor this means considering your own expectations of tutoring and of the personal interaction between tutor and student. What do you consider your role as a personal tutor to be? What is the role of the student both as a tutee and as a learner? How and when do you expect a student to approach you for assistance? What issues do you feel are within your remit as a personal tutor? An examination of your own attitudes and beliefs should also include your expectations about how students will engage in tutorials.

It is necessary for tutors to be aware of these expectations because it is against these that, consciously or unconsciously, they will judge students. Where students do not meet expectations there is a danger that a tutor may

Case Study

One of the biggest challenges is ensuring that you are not making assumptions about a student's understanding of a situation. I remember one female student, who was from the Middle East and had mobility difficulties. There had been a lot of planning for her starting the course, the department had just moved into a new building where access was a problem and we were aware that she would be living and studying in the UK for the first time. When she first started the course, I was given responsibility for ensuring the access issues were addressed so I told her to let me know if she had any problems or questions. At first there were some problems with access that needed to be ironed out and some other small administrative issues came up, which I normally wouldn't handle but did in this case since I was already chasing the access issues. I only ever intended to give this extra time for a week or two, just until the access issues had been ironed out and she had settled in. It took about three weeks to make the changes needed for access, but even after that was done she kept coming to see me almost every day, to ask questions she should have been speaking to her course tutors about and sometimes it seemed it was just to chat. I became quite frustrated and just could not understand why she was being so demanding.

It took a colleague to point out to me that the student might not be intending to be demanding. He suggested that she perhaps didn't understand the role of a personal tutor. I'd never spoken to her about personal tutoring and we don't really talk about the role of a personal tutor during induction. I guess I had just expected that she would understand that the support I was giving her at the start of the session was exceptional and only really to resolve the access problems. I realised that it was unrealistic to expect someone from another country and culture and with no experience of university in this country to automatically understand the situation.

I took the opportunity to sit down with the student and talk about the roles of course tutors and personal tutor. It quickly became clear that she hadn't seen the difference. In talking to her, I was also surprised to discover her expectations about pastoral care. She assumed that she would be getting a lot of personal support from the academic staff and particularly from me. I think she felt a bit hurt or rejected when I explained that her expectations were unrealistic. Our relationship was a bit uncomfortable from then on. I think things would have been different if I'd been clear from the start about my role.

attribute this to a deficiency on the student's part. A tutor who believes punctuality is important, for example, may consider a student who comes late to tutorials without explanation to be disorganised or disrespectful. Whilst it is natural for all human beings to feel negatively about other people who act differently from their expectations, in a multi-cultural environment this can create unnecessary barriers.

The second aspect of developing multi-cultural competence requires the understanding and acceptance that others will hold different values and beliefs from yours. This does not mean that one's own beliefs should be abandoned, nor that the beliefs of others must take precedence. Rather, it means that difference should be openly acknowledged and discussed.

The Centre for Teaching and Learning at the University of Minnesota (2006) has published a list of areas where there might be disparity of value/belief between students and their academic advisers. The British Council, in *Feeling at Home* (Hughes and Hardy, 2002) also discusses a number of aspects of culture which can be problematic in tutor/student relationships if they are not understood. These include different understandings of the nature of truth, the relative importance of education and family and different rules of conversation. Effective tutors need to be willing to engage in a dialogue with students about expectations and to acknowledge alternative views and approaches.

It must be recognised that this second aspect of multi-cultural competence may be the most difficult to enact for personal tutors as it requires the tutor to take the time to discuss with students the beliefs and values which underpin behaviour. To the over-worked tutor it is much easier to just tell a student to arrive promptly next time rather than to spend 20 minutes discussing with a student why they might feel it is acceptable to come late for an appointment. However, the former approach does not enable either the student or the tutor to understand the other's point of view or to consider new ways of working which would be mutually acceptable.

There can be a significant impact to student learning when personal tutors dismiss the issues arising from difference. A recent study into care leavers in higher education (Jackson et al., 2005) found that many staff in higher education believed that care leavers were not of a sufficient standard to benefit from higher education. However, the research showed that the key difficulties for the students were the results of gaps in previous learning caused by their unsettled past, complicated family situations and inappropriate coping strategies. There was no evidence that students leaving care were less able than other students, but rather they were shown to have had additional difficulties which were not recognised by tutors. Other research into part-time students reflected similar problems with lack of understanding

(Universities UK, 2006). The research showed that 38 per cent of the students felt that academic staff did not recognise the pressure they were under combining employment and study, and 36 per cent felt that inadequate support and advice was a barrier to their participation.

Having discussed the need for personal tutors to consider and address diversity in personal terms of difference, it may still be useful to consider a few areas where differences can be particularly sensitive. The British Council publishes a guide for working with international students (Hughes and Hardy, 2002) and the Inter Faith Network publishes a short guide for working with those from other faith traditions (2005). Both discuss some areas for general awareness that it may be useful to touch on here.

Physical contact

One area, which is very likely to elicit quite strong responses when cultural conflict occurs, is touching. There are widely different ideas between individuals and groups as to what constitutes acceptable physical contact between an academic staff member and a student and between men and women. Within British society handshakes and touching on the arm or shoulder, a clap on the back for example, are generally seen as acceptable between a tutor and student of any gender. However, there are students from a number of groups who would find physical contact unacceptable. Some Islamic students, students from Middle and Far Eastern cultural traditions and survivors of physical assault, rape or abuse could find even minor physical contact distressing.

This is not to say that personal tutors should totally refrain from physical contact, rather that they should think carefully about how well they know a student and how sure they are that the student will not mind contact.

Names

The use of names is a second area where individuals can have strong feelings and may respond quite severely when differences arise. It is important for personal tutors to ensure that they call students by the name the students prefer and with which they are comfortable. Some international students may choose to use an English name, if this is their choice then it needs to be respected. Tutors should ask students how they wish to be addressed, and follow their wishes. Students can be made uncomfortable when staff insist on acting against their preferences when it comes to names. Even when well intentioned, using a formal form of address or their registered name can make a student feel uncomfortable. Giving students nicknames is a practice best avoided, as it is likely to make some students uncomfortable and in some cases may cause serious offence.

Assumptions

Personal tutors should be conscious of the need to avoid making assumptions about students' life outside of the university. As discussed above, students may have very different beliefs and values and as a result can have difficulty being understood by academic staff. In making incorrect assumptions about students' circumstances, personal tutors give evidence to those students that they and their situation are not understood. Even relatively minor comments can inadvertently alienate students. Personal tutors, when offering advice or guidance, should never make assumptions about the context of the student's life. It is not appropriate to assume a student has a family on which they can rely for assistance or that their family is supportive of their studies. Age is no longer a good indicator of whether a student might have dependants and not every student would favour a heterosexual relationship. Where it is relevant to advising students, personal tutors need to ask them about their personal circumstances.

Learning experiences

Finally, when considering how to advise students it is important for tutors to provide alternative options whereever possible. It is natural for personal tutors to share their own experiences, and the methods of learning and problem solving which they have found successful. However, there can be a danger that tutors give students the impression that only individuals like themselves can be successful academically. The Centre for Instructional Development and Research (CIDR, 2006), in their guide to working with students in a multi-cultural environment, have included student comments about their learning experiences. Several of these comments reflect the disquiet students feel when academic staff are reflective of only a single pathway to academic success. One student in particular questions what is seen to be an assumption that students desire to be like their tutors, and indeed must become like them to achieve academic success. In an environment of diversity it is important to enable students, as far as possible, to find their own pathways and define academic success in their own terms. This may mean sharing with students not only your own approach to resolving problems, but also alternative methods that have worked for colleagues or other students. It means accepting that some students will not measure academic success by the level of their degree award or even in the attainment of a degree.

● Diversity and student mental health

Student diversity in higher education is complex and is likely to affect many aspects of a student's experience, not just their relationship with their personal tutor. Personal tutors need to be aware that issues of difference which affect other aspects of a student's life may have implications for personal tutoring. Diversity may have a profound impact on the ability of some students to interact with their peers or to engage in the student social community. Research at the University of Leicester into student mental health in 1998 (Grant, 2002) found that students from ethnic minority groups had higher levels of distress than their white peers. A related study into mental health and student drinking (Grant, 2004) found similarly a greater level of mental distress amongst students who did not drink, whether from ethnic minority groups or white. The increase in distress amongst ethnic minority students and in non-drinking students was attributed, at least in part, to some isolation from other students. Where students are unable to form links with other students for any reason, they are likely to be missing out on a strong source of support. This may therefore increase the importance for them of sensitive support from a personal tutor.

Referral
The complicated lives of some students can mean that personal tutors are faced with student issues that they feel are beyond their remit or for which specialist support is more appropriate. In these instances, it is critical that tutors are able to refer students on to other services and facilities appropriately. All universities will have some provision for assisting students with personal and practical problems. These services most often include things such as accommodation, financial support, welfare, careers advice and disability services. However, the particular mix of services and their organisation is unique to each university. Personal tutors need to be fully aware of the particular suite of support services available within their own institution as well as details of when and how they can be accessed.

For many students, the way in which a referral to another service is made is as important as the referral itself. Students who may already be receiving negative messages about their place within the university community because of their difference can find the referral process to be a negative experience. It can have a very negative impact on students where personal tutors give the message that their problems have no relevance to the academic environment, or worse, that their problems somehow make them unsuitable for continuing in education. What is needed is for the personal tutor to acknowledge the impact personal issues are having on the student's learning and to adopt an attitude of collaboration, both with the student and with support services, in addressing the issue. This is not to say that there may not be circumstances where problems are so serious as to make inter-mitting or withdrawing from study the best course of action. However, students are often able to deal successfully with significant problems with a combination of appropriate specialist support and understanding from their personal and course tutors.

● Personal conflict

Finally, it would be remiss to consider diversity without mentioning the conflict that it can sometimes create. There may be circumstances where dealing with diversity can be personally challenging. Where a student's

A student approached the Student Services Welfare Adviser about the process for changing her personal tutor. When asked about the reason for wanting to change, the student burst into tears and explained that she found that it had become almost impossible to even speak to her personal tutor. The student had gender dysphoria and was in the process of gender reassignment from a male to a female identity. After much consideration, she had decided to disclose this to staff as she believed that some of the side effects of the medication and medical procedures might have an impact on her studies at times. She was aware that some people might be uncomfortable with her particular condition, but in disclosing she had antici-pated that it would result in better understanding and a sympathetic response should she have absences.

Whilst some staff had seemed to be unaffected by this disclosure, she felt that her personal tutor was exceptionally uncomfortable with this infor-mation and with her. When meeting with her tutor, he sat as far away from her as possible with his arms and legs crossed. He avoided any close contact and always claimed to be very busy whenever she came to speak to him. She was exceptionally frustrated and angry that she was unable to get any real assistance from him. Instead she found that when she went to see him his behaviour was so extreme as to completely distract her from the reason she went to see him, and his desire to end the meeting as quickly as possible meant that she received inadequate advice and support.

What she found even more difficult was her tutor's failure to even admit that there was a problem. When she had suggested that he might prefer for her to change to another personal tutor he had dismissed this idea and insisted that he was happy to act as her personal tutor. She felt trapped in a situation where she either had to accept poor support from her personal tutor or go over his head to force a change.

personal beliefs clash with your own moral or ethical beliefs it can be difficult to retain enough detachment to remain effective as an advisor. As discussed earlier, it is unrealistic to keep personal issues out of personal tutoring, therefore there may be occasions when tutors learn about aspects of a student's life which they find disturbing. Issues such as forced marriage, abortion, homosexuality, gender reassignment or militant political or religious views may come to light. Where this happens, it can be difficult for a tutor to find a way to support the student that is comfortable and productive.

Where a student expresses beliefs that are directly challenging to a tutor's own views the tutor needs to be honest with the student about their discomfort. It is advisable to be open in discussing your discomfort or the fact that you hold values that conflict with those of the student. Depending on the situation, it may be possible through this discussion to find ways to continue to support the student. In some circumstances, however, the issues presented may be so contentious or emotional that dialogue may not be enough to enable a comfortable working relationship between tutor and student. In these circumstances the student should be consulted as to possible alternative arrangements. As such situations can be very stressful and even potentially litigious, it is advisable to consider at a departmental or institutional level how issues of incompatibility are to be managed, in advance of any situation arising.

Practical suggestions

☐ Any concerns raised by students about behaviour that makes them feel distressed, uncomfortable or embarrassed should be taken seriously.

☐ Be familiar with your university's discrimination and harassment policies.

☐ Be familiar with your institution's equality action plans and OFFA access agreement.

☐ Be clear in your own mind about your own expectations of personal tutoring.

☐ Discuss with students their understanding or expectations.

☐ Be aware of the discomfort that can be caused by physical contact.

☐ Ask students for their preferred form of address.

☐ Be alert to assumptions about a student's personal circumstances.

☐ Be familiar with the support services within your institution so that you can make referrals.

☐ Consider in advance what steps you might take when confronted with issues that you find ethically or morally challenging.

● Further reading

Association of University Administrators (AUA) Higher Education Equal Opportunities Network (HEEON) and Equality Challenge Unit (ECU) (March 2005), *A–Z Equality and Diversity* (London: AUA, HEEON and ECU).

Centre for Instructional Development and Research (CIDR), University of Washington (online) (2006), www.depts.washington.edu/cidrweb/inclusive/background.html (accessed on 7 November 2006).

Centre for Media, Arts and Performance, Coventry School of Art and Design, Coventry University (2006), *Same but Different: Working Effectively with Student Diversity* (DVD Training Resource pack), Coventry University.

Centre for Teaching and Learning (CTL), University of Minnesota (online) (2006), *Cultural/Ethnic Disparity in Advising*, available from: www.umn.edu/ohr/teachlearn/resources/diversity/advising.html (accessed 7 November 2006).

Department for Education and Skills (online) (17 November 2006), *Guidance for Higher Education Providers to Help Tackle Violent Extremism in the Name of Islam on Campus*, available from: www.dfes.gov.uk/pns/pnaattach/20060170/1.txt (accessed 18 November 2006).

Equality Challenge Unit (ECU) (November 2004), *Equality is Challenging . . . Positive Action* (London, ECU).

Equality Challenge Unit (August 2005), *Equal Opportunities: An Introduction* (London, ECU).

Grant, A. (2002), 'Identifying Students' Concerns', in N. Stanley and J.

Manthorpe (eds), *Students' Mental Health Needs: Problems and Responses* (London: Jessica Kingsley).

Grant, A. (2004), 'Alcohol and Student Success', *Association for University and College Counselling Journal* (Winter), 18–21.

Hughes, R. and Hardey, J. (2002), *Feeling at Home*, 3rd edn (London: British Council).

Inter-Faith Network for the United Kingdom (2005), *Building Good Relations with People of Different Faiths and Beliefs* (London: Inter-Faith Network for the UK).

Jackson, S., Ajayi, S. and Quigley, M, (2005), *Going to University from Care* (London: Institute of Education, University of London and Frank Buttle Trust).

Trevithick, P. (2003), 'Overcoming Educational Disadvantage', *Association for University and College Counselling Journal* (Winter), 2–6.

7 Counselling Support for the Student and Personal Tutor

Elizabeth Hewitt

This chapter will explore the range of undergraduate support services that exist in higher educaton institutions to support both the personal tutor and his/her work with tutees. It will explore the interface between the personal tutor and the student counselling service, discussing the possible expectations institutions hold of a counselling service, the issue of confidentiality, and the support that a counselling service can offer to a tutor. The chapter ends with a section on the skills of referral, offering practical ideas for developing effective communication between the tutor and other student support services, clues which indicate a need to refer, and guidelines on how to make an effective referral.

● Introduction

My experience of personal tutoring began over twenty-five years ago when I started work in the educational sector. I have been a personal tutor in both colleges of higher education and secondary schools, and, in the latter, I was for several years the leader of a team of personal tutors. It was always apparent that the tutorial relationship exists within, is affected by, and hopefully, gains support from the institution of which it is a part. Now, as a Senior Counsellor at the University of Worcester, I recognise that the interface between the personal tutor and the other parts of the institution remains significant for a successful tutor/tutee relationship, and requires both awareness and attention from both sides. From my own experience, and from observation, I know how helpful the tutorial relationship can be to a student, and I also know how hard it can be to balance the demands of the role with the other expectations the institution has of the tutor.

In this chapter the role of the personal tutor will be placed within the context of the wider support systems that are available for a student. These wider support systems are to be found in all HE institutions under a range of titles such as Student Services, or Student Life and Development, and are aimed at supporting the students while encouraging their growing independence during this life stage. The range of services usually offered under such a remit will be reviewed. The particular interface between the personal tutor and a counselling service will be explored, focusing on what a counselling service can offer to both tutor and tutee. The importance of referring students on to other types of support, a necessary part of the personal tutor's role, will be addressed, and guidelines will be offered for effective use of the skill of referral.

The personal tutor can often feel isolated and unsupported, in a role which can sometimes be very time consuming, and yet may seem to be unacknowledged. It is therefore especially important that he/she is aware of, and can draw on, other areas of student support. To use these areas of support effectively, and to enable tutees to do so, requires both the knowledge of what is available in the institution (Wheeler and Birtle, 1993, p. 122), and the skills of referral.

Feelings of pressure and isolation, which tutors can experience from time to time as they try to do their best for their tutees, can be reduced if the tutor bears in mind that he/she is a part, not the whole, of the wider support system available for students in their institution. Knowing what Student Services offer, and how what is offered can be accessed, contributes to this sense of being part of that wider support system. The range of services available, and where they can be found, will vary from institution to institution, but will usually include careers advice, welfare and finance advice, learning support tutors, programme/module advisers, the international office, a medical centre, spiritual support, mental health advisers, and the student counselling service. Each will have its own particular areas of expertise with which to support students, and they will now be briefly reviewed.

● The range of available support services

Careers service

The careers service is usually available to all current students of the institution, and often to students who have graduated within the last three years, in some cases also those who graduated from other institutions. Careers advisers encourage students to visit the service early in their university life, rather than waiting until they are about to graduate. The careers service provides access to information about different careers, and about further vocational and postgraduate courses. There will be computer-aided guidance software packages such as Prospects, and perhaps Adult Directions, Exodus and Funderfinder, to enable students to do their own research about choices they are considering.

Students can have one-to-one advice from qualified careers advisers, through an appointment system, or 'drop-in' sessions. Often workshops, as well as individual help, are available where students will be helped to decide what they want to do, to plan the best route into their chosen career, to write an effective CV, to make job applications and to prepare for interviews or selection centres. Most careers services will work with academic departments to raise students' awareness of employability issues and this will underpin the personal development planning (PDP) process. Many HE careers services hold careers fairs or employer presentations, at which prospective graduates can meet potential employers. They will usually also advertise local and national job vacancies, including opportunities for part-time and vacation work, and possibly, placements. A number of careers services have their own dedicated employer liaison departments.

Welfare and finance advice

Students can access welfare and financial advice provided by the university. There may be an appointment and/or a 'drop-in' system. Students will be given help to access financial support while at university, such as loans and grants, and they will be supported in completing relevant forms. The finance advisers may administer discretionary funds, such as the Access to Learning Fund, and any other short-term funds/loans which may be available. They will also have information about funding for further courses. Information provided by students is treated in confidence.

The welfare and finance adviser can provide advice regarding budgeting, welfare benefits and debt-management. If necessary, she may liaise with creditors on the student's behalf, and give the students advice to help them to restructure their debts. Should a student's personal circumstances change, perhaps when a relationship breaks down and the student is newly single, the adviser can help with the financial implications of the altered circumstances.

Sasha had always wanted to study for a degree. She was now in her early thirties and was a single parent. She was receiving welfare benefits and was trying to pay off debts, and was concerned that she would not be able to afford to go to university.

She spoke to the university's welfare and finance adviser at an Open Day. He told her about the various loans and grants which could be available to her, including the Childcare Grant and the Parents' Learning Allowance. Sasha realised that her income would not be reduced by receiving these.

When she had enrolled, the welfare and finance adviser helped her to negotiate with her creditors to have her repayments reduced until after she had graduated.

Later in the year, her car, on which she depended to get to university, needed expensive repairs. She was able to apply for help from her university's Access to Learning Fund, and received a grant which enabled her to pay for the repairs and thus continue at university.

Disability and learning support

This area of student support may be part of a Student Services remit or may be found under a different heading. Students who suspect they have a specific learning difficulty, such as dyslexia, can be offered screening and assessment by qualified staff. Experienced tutors will provide specialist academic support in appropriately equipped rooms, often on a weekly basis.

Students with visual and hearing impairment will likewise be offered specialist academic support, such as a taping service (transferring text to tape), a brailling service, interpreters and lip speakers, as well as the loan of specialised equipment such as dictaphones or hearing loops. Students can be further supported on their courses by scribes, note-takers, readers and proof-readers. Many of these services will be directly funded through the Disabled Student's Allowance, rather than being freely available to all students. Learning support centres also usually offer specialised awareness training workshops for tutors, teaching staff and peer groups.

Programme/module advisers

Not all institutions have programme advisers, especially if they do not have a module degree scheme. In the case of institutions where many students do follow a modular degree scheme, programme advisers may be departmentally based, or may be organised on an institution-wide basis in order to represent the whole degree programme to students. In this latter case, departments will also continue to offer advice to students about modules in their subject areas.

Programme advisers may be departmentally based, especially where an institution does not have a modular scheme for its degrees, but, in the case of institutions where many students do follow a modular scheme, they may be organised on an institution-wide basis in order to represent the whole degree programme to students. In this case departments will also continue to offer advice to students about modules in their subject areas.

Programme advisers ensure that students select modules which conform to the regulations required by their degree course, and that they use the flexibility which is a part of modular schemes to make choices that reflect particular interests. When students need to re-organise their degree programmes, because of retakes, illness, or other unforeseen circumstances, programme advisers can ensure that the chosen courses, while being do-able from the student's perspective, continue to meet the requirements of their degree. Most programme advisory services offer 'drop-in' times as well as appointments.

International office

In some institutions the International Office may be mainly involved in recruitment but many also see their role as one of offering support to those students whom they have recruited while they are studying at their institution.

So the International Office may see itself as supporting international students from their first enquiry and application through to graduation. Many have strong links with institutions in the countries from which students come, and will be clearly aware of cultural differences and differing expectations regarding university life. They can give advice about courses which are specifically tailored for international students, such as introductory courses which help to prepare a student for study at a British university, and language skills courses for those who may be struggling with English. They may also organise special induction programmes for international students, social activities, and individual support, possibly through a 'buddying' scheme.

The International Office offers ongoing individual and practical support to students during their time away from home while studying at your institution. They will give advice regarding immigration status, and regarding the possibilities for employment while at university. They may help with getting accommodation while at university, often liaising with the Accommodation Office or landlords on the student's behalf. When a student needs to return home unexpectedly, the International Office can help to arrange flights.

Matthew was a Chinese undergraduate student. When he arrived at university, the adviser in the International Office was able to help him in the first days with arranging a bank account and registering with the local GP practice. She also helped him to register with the police, which, as a student from China, he had to do within seven days of his arrival.

His tutor contacted the International Office a few weeks into the term, concerned that Matthew's English was letting him down. The adviser there discussed with Matthew what would be helpful, and then arranged for him to have extra English classes in the Language Unit. She also put him in contact with a fellow student who was a volunteer in the university's buddying scheme, so that he could practise his English conversation.

When, at the end of the first year, Matthew's visa was running out, he was helped to renew it by the International Office adviser.

Spiritual support

The role of the chaplain, and the extent of their embeddedness within the institution, can vary, often for historical reasons. The more ancient universities, and those institutions which began life as Colleges of Education may well have been Christian foundations, and they will probably continue to have a purpose-built chapel, and a chaplain who has always held a recognised role, both formal, and informal, in the life of the institution. In the more recent universities, there is more likely to be a chaplaincy centre, and the part played by the chaplain within the institution may not be so clear, and may be a part-time, or shared, appointment between different Christian denominations (Church of England Report, 2005).

The numbers of international students and of those from ethnic minority backgrounds have grown in recent years, and consequently there is a need for any spiritual provision to reflect the diversity of faiths. In some institutions, inter-faith centres provide pastoral and spiritual support to meet the needs of the whole community, offering appropriate places for worship and meditation, as well as spiritual leaders who can respond to the concerns of students wishing to remain within their faith tradition while at university.

Chaplains and other religious leaders may have a formal role in providing religious services, but they can also have an informal role. Their very presence within the institution offers the potential for a different kind of support to students. They are independent of the institution, and can meet students in ways which may not be easily open to other support services. Their being simply 'around' in the Students' Union may give students a first opportunity to speak with someone who is comfortable in discussing matters of faith.

Students who are facing distressing events in their lives, which may call into question their previously held views, may find conversations with a spiritual adviser from within their own faith tradition helpful. Chaplains, and other religious leaders, also have the freedom to respond to those students who feel isolated by offering them a faith community to be a part of, and inviting them to meet others with similar views and values in a social context. When institutional or wider tragedies occur, the chaplain and other spiritual leaders provide the rituals which facilitate the grieving process and support both individuals and the community.

Medical centre

The provision made to meet the health needs of students varies, and many institutions have more recently chosen to limit the scope of health services on offer to students. An institution may have a contract with a local GP practice, to have a GP providing surgeries on campus, or an arrangement through which students can register with the local practice while at the university. Many medical centres will still be staffed by a qualified nurse. They can help students to register with the GP. They deal with 'first aid' matters, such as changing dressings. They will respond to emergencies on campus, and often support students who have been ill and are recovering, especially those in Halls who, for whatever reason, cannot go home. Most medical centres have a 'recovery room' where students (or staff) suffering from, for example, ME, sickness or migraine, can rest under supervision.

Medical centre staff may arrange for specialist medical advice services to be available on campus in areas such as Sexual Health. They may run health campaigns for issues such as smoking, drinking, and meningitis awareness. They provide reassurance to students worried about their health, give advice when necessary about further medical help, and are usually skilled listeners. In some institutions the medical centre may provide or arrange occupational health services for staff.

Mental health advisers

When an institution has mental health advisers, students are automatically referred to them if they reveal on their application to university that they have a mental health problem, but it is up to the student, as an adult, to make use of the support they offer. If a student appears to be behaving in ways which seem out of character, or bizarre, it may be that that student's personal tutor would find a discussion with one of the mental health advisers helpful in determining the appropriateness of a referral.

Some of the issues mental health advisers work with in students are psychotic behaviour/thoughts (where the student seems to have lost touch with reality), extreme anxiety, clinical depression, bi-polar disorder, attention deficit hyper-activity disorder, autistic spectrum disorders such as Asperger's syndrome, obsessive compulsive disorder, eating disorders, body dysmorphia and self-harm. All of these conditions have a negative effect on a student's ability to meet the demands of university life. Some students need support to deal with their condition throughout the whole of their university career, while others are able to manage successfully after a briefer period of support from the mental health adviser.

Mental health advisers are qualified mental health nurses. The service can normally be accessed through appointments, with emergency slots available if necessary. Information the student shares is confidential unless the student gives specific consent to its disclosure. Mental health advisers will give advice to a student about their need to see, for example, a GP or a psychiatrist. They may help them to make an appointment, and even take them to it if they feel that otherwise the student would not attend. They may liaise, with the student's agreement, with a student's parents, and/or social workers or Community Mental Health teams from the student's home area, especially if the student needs support when away from university during holiday periods. If a student is socially withdrawn, and perhaps struggling to leave their room, the mental health adviser may visit them in halls or their lodgings, and perhaps go out with them for an informal chat over a cup of coffee, and help them to become more comfortable when moving around the campus. They will help a student to complete mitigating circumstances' forms, and provide required evidence to support a claim.

> A full-time mature student with a long history of clinical depression, Rachel had very low self-esteem and suffered panic attacks. She felt that she was not intelligent enough to be a student on a degree course, but she had wanted to do it for some time, to prove to herself and others that she is intelligent. She had completed her first year of an English degree success-fully. But she was finding it hard juggling her studies with being a mother to two young children.
>
> Her personal tutor was understanding and supportive of her as a mature student, but Rachel had not liked to disclose her history of mental illness to her. Her tutor, recognising that Rachel seemed anxious at times, mentioned the availability of support in Student Services if she was feeling stressed, and gave her some leaflets. In this way Rachel found out about the existence of the mental health advisers, and made an appointment.
>
> While Rachel came across as confident, always smiling, and appeared to be in control, this was far from the truth: in reality she felt inadequate and unworthy, always tired, mainly due to keeping up this façade. With her mental health adviser, Rachel was able to be open about how she really felt; she could let down the façade, and explore her real feelings. The mental health adviser helped her to monitor her moods and to manage them more effectively for herself, using a range of techniques and small life-style changes.

● Student counselling service

All HE institutions, and most FE institutions, now have a student counselling service. Some services are placed within Student Services, and others may be part of the Students' Union, or stand alone as a separate service. All current students have access to the service, which is free, confidential and is staffed by qualified counsellors. The ways in which students can make an appointment may vary, but it is usual for at least a first appointment to be made within a matter of days. At peak times of demand, there may be a waiting list, but services normally have spaces available for emergency appointments. Many services offer an initial number of sessions, perhaps up to six 50-minute sessions, or more. But where students need more time to work on their issues, most services are able to respond to that need, and would see it as ethically right to do so. In practice, many students require fewer than six sessions with their counsellor.

Counselling offers a place where the student will be listened to in a safe, private and uninterrupted space, somewhere to talk in confidence to a qualified counsellor who is not a friend, but someone quite separate from the rest of the student's life. The counsellor will not give advice, or tell the student what to do. Rather, she will facilitate the students' making their own choices, as they decide what to talk about, and as they express their concerns, without judgement. Counselling offers to the student a supportive environment in which he/she can work to make whatever changes he/she sees as needed to help him/her to live in a more effective and fulfilling way.

> Pete was referred to the Counselling Service by his tutor because his mood had appeared to change in class, and he was looking especially unkempt. He had stopped attending lectures regularly, and his tutor was concerned for him.
>
> Working with his counsellor over several weeks, Pete began to identify the reasons for his change in mood and behaviour. His longstanding partner, whom he had met soon after he came to England, had recently ended the relationship, and Pete had begun to drink quite heavily to avoid his feelings. He explored with his counsellor the extent of his loss: not only had he lost his partner, but also her family, who had 'adopted' him as their own, and given him something his own family had not been able to give from so far away. He began to realise that he was grieving for several losses, and that his feelings were a natural response.
>
> Being able to understand his feelings enabled Pete to accept them, rather than try to blot them out with alcohol. He began to get back in touch with friends and slowly regained his motivation for his academic work, and started to realise that he did still have a future.

● The interface between the personal tutor and the counselling service

The interface between the personal tutor's role and that of the counsellor in the student counselling service can often be a source of concern for both parties (Bell, 1996; Hewitt and Wheeler, 2004; May, 1999). Tutors may be unsure about what a counselling service can offer, and when to refer a student, and can at times find the boundaries placed by counsellors around the counselling relationship frustrating. There may be expectations held by the institution about counselling which the counselling service is unable or unwilling to meet.

A common expectation is that if a student goes for counselling all will be well, the student will be enabled to stay on their course and complete their studies – in part because of a belief that counselling 'sorts people out' and makes them better. But this can create tension, as well as risk to the service, especially if the student, despite having counselling, does not 'improve', and does not begin to cope more effectively with college demands. It may be that the student will decide that leaving the course is, for them, at that time, the best option, but the expectation of the academic staff may have been that the outcome of counselling would be not only that the student not only stayed on their course but also that the counselling service would be able to transform the student and his or her situation almost instantly.

Noonan (1983) describes this expectation as attributing to the counsellor some 'magical quality' which will 'defy reality' (p. 139). This particular situation highlights the risk of being seen to fail to achieve the outcome desired by the institution, even if counselling had provided the student with the space to make a decision and so, from the student's point of view, it was a satisfactory outcome. It raises questions for the counsellor, and tutors, like 'what is a successful outcome in counselling?' and 'What do others expect when they refer a student to counselling?'

A particular ethical challenge to a counselling service concerns the perception of the counsellor as a useful player in the area of discipline. Counsellors are very concerned that the disciplinary procedures of the institution should be quite separate from the student's attendance for counselling (Shea and Bond, 1997). But it can happen that students can be 'sent' to counselling who may be in danger of suspension, in the hope that the counselling process will 'reform' the student. The motivation behind this request/ demand may be mixed: recognition that here is a student in need of support and a wish to do something to alleviate the anxiety felt in the face of such need, as well as a desire that someone else solve an awkward problem. The voluntary nature of counselling, and respect for the client's autonomy, may be ethical issues which tutor or management may never have considered.

Further difficulties can arise when the counsellor is expected to support both student and college in the system of extensions and or mitigating circumstances. It is not unreasonable for a naturally anxious tutor to encourage a student to 'go to see the counsellor' when faced with someone who is in danger of failing and in need of an extension. From a counsellor's point of view, if this suggestion is linked with a possibility of the immediate provision of a letter of evidence by the counsellor, it becomes a contentious issue (Gilbert, 1989; Warburton, 1995). Counselling services will respond differently to requests to support the 'mitigating circumstances' system through letters of evidence. Most will have a policy governing how they will respond. Generally, counsellors are unwilling to provide letters of evidence if they have not seen a student previously for counselling. But where a student has used the service, and therefore the counsellor has been aware of the student's difficulties, the student will be required to sign a consent to the disclosure of any information, and will agree with the counsellor what they both think needs to be said in a letter of evidence.

Counsellors' insistence on confidentiality concerning their clients can be found to be, in varying degrees, frustrating by many members of staff, especially tutors. Confidentiality is regarded by counsellors as a very significant boundary around the counselling relationship. Most services will have a written policy on confidentiality which is given to clients at the time of their making a first appointment for counselling. This confidentiality extends even to whether or not a student is actually attending counselling, and counsellors make it clear to clients that it is up to them, not the counsellor, who they choose to tell that they are indeed attending counselling. This can sometimes be seen by tutors (who are, of course, acting out of concern for their students) wanting to know that they have come for help, as the counsellor being precious and needlessly awkward. But it is a way in which respect for the client's autonomy, and the client's right to confidentiality in dealing with very personal issues, can be demonstrated very clearly.

While counsellors see their primary role as providing one-to-one counselling for students, and if the service is so resourced, for staff too, they also recognise that a further important aspect of their role can be described as supporting the 'supporters', and in this sense the counselling service can be used as a wider college resource. The counsellor is in a particular position to give advice and to contain anxieties, and most services welcome contacts from tutors working with their tutees who want what could be called one-to-one *sounding board* consultations, in which the tutor's fears and concerns about working with a particular student could be talked through, and further possible ways to do so can be discussed. In this way, the counsellor will seek to support the tutor so that he/she can continue to work with their student with increased confidence.

Protecting other staff from the potentially overwhelming anxiety of feeling responsible for distressed students is a significant task of the student counsellor (May, 1999). Bell (1997) suggests that the counsellor, by providing information through workshops for staff about the signs of disturbance and about what can be done, can help to contain anxiety and in this way support staff in continuing to support the student. So, many counselling services, if staffing resources allow, will offer workshops on supporting students with particular issues, such as eating disorders, anxiety, self-harm, and those experiencing loss and grief. They may also offer workshops on basic listening skills, and how and when to refer students elsewhere.

● The skills of referral

Knowledge about the further range of support services available to students is a necessary part of the role of the personal tutor. As a personal tutor, you are not required to be an expert in everything, to be fully aware of financial matters, to be able to give careers advice, to counsel a student in emotional distress. There are other services available with that expertise, and knowing where they are, and what they can offer, so that you can refer your tutee appropriately, is the sign of an effective tutor (Grant, 2006).

Ways to develop communication between yourself as tutor and other support services
To equip yourself for this aspect of your role, there are some basic ways in which communication between you and other support services can be facilitated.

- Find out where Student Services, or its equivalent in your institution, is on campus, so that you can tell a tutee where to find the specific support they might need.
- Check out the range of services available, perhaps by contacting the Student Services Information Desk, or the Head of Student Services, or by looking on the Student Services web pages. Most student support services would welcome your interest, and be willing to spend time explaining what they offer.
- Most services have leaflets detailing what they offer and how they can be contacted; ask for a stock of leaflets for your information, but also so that you can give them to your tutees when suggesting a referral.
- Have a list of contact numbers and email addresses handy, so that you can discuss the appropriateness of possible referrals, perhaps even before you suggest them to a student.
- Suggest that an agenda item for your next departmental meeting could be an invitation to the Head of Student Services to talk about the range of student support available in your institution and how it can be accessed.
- Avail yourself of any opportunities for continuing professional development by finding out which of the services offer workshops for tutors, e.g. disability and learning support offering awareness training; the International Office offering cultural awareness workshops; the counselling service offering workshops on listening skills, and on dealing with distressed students.

It is a skill in itself to recognise the need for referral, and to achieve a successful referral (Wheeler and Birtle, 1993, p. 50). Lago and Shipton (1994, p. 78) discuss different reasons for referral. Some referrals may be related to the needs of the tutor as much as to those of their tutee. The tutor may feel unable to deal with the issues the tutee brings, perhaps because they recognise that the tutee needs more time than the tutor has available, or because the tutor feels anxious about coping helpfully with the tutee's difficulty, or because the tutor simply feels 'out of their depth' in dealing with an issue which may even be 'too close to home'.

All of the above are good reasons to refer a student on. But the value for students of simply having a place to which they can come in order to discuss any issues without repercussions on the rest of their college life is often underestimated (Thomas, 2006). It is for this reason that an appropriate and timely referral may well be a most helpful aspect of the tutor's role. Personal tutors write students' references, so students may not want to talk about personal problems because there may be a perceived conflict there. So it is important that students have a neutral place to come to, a place separate from the academic arena. Other support services, too, especially the mental health advisers or the student counselling service, can provide an independent, neutral place where students can go to discuss their problems.

The relief felt by students in having a separate place entirely away from academic demands, to explore their personal concerns, as well as the relief of tutors who then do not have to involve themselves in such issues, is mentioned by Bell (1997). McLeod (1999) attributes the counsellor's value to the student precisely as being her separateness, in that she is not involved in the academic tasks with which the rest of the institution is concerned, and can, therefore, explore issues which are not part of the 'official' discourse of the institution. So, helping a tutee to access other means of support is an appropriate, and significant, aspect of the personal tutor's role.

Guidance on when to refer a tutee on to other services
Most students when they come to their personal tutor will be seeking support, advice or information, sometimes of an academic nature, but sometimes also about other, more personal or specific issues. Deciding when to refer is not always easy or clear-cut, but there are certain clues which may suggest to you as tutor that referring the student on is an appropriate option. These include:

- When a student does not seem to be coping with day-to-day responsibilities and activities: they may not be going to lectures, or to their job; their academic performance generally, or their grades, may have dropped.

- When a student does not seem to have a support network, family or friends with whom they can talk about whatever is troubling them.
- When a student tells you that they are suffering from sleep disturbance, fatigue, inability to concentrate on anything, social withdrawal, tearfulness, sudden weight loss or gain (these symptoms can indicate depression).
- When you observe that the student is unusually unkempt in appearance, failing to take care with personal hygiene, not bothering about their clothes, and that this is different from how they have presented themselves previously.
- When a student tells you that they feel stressed: that they are often 'panicky', breathless, have headaches, a dry mouth, sweaty palms, their thoughts are chaotic (all symptoms of anxiety).
- When a student tells you that there doesn't seem much point in anything any more, and they might as well end it – thoughts of suicide.
- **A Rule of Thumb: if you feel overwhelmed or unusually anxious in response to your tutee, consider referral.**

Guidance on how to make an effective referral

Apart from knowing when a referral could be appropriate, there are also guidelines which can make referral an informed and positive choice, and therefore one from which your tutee is most likely to benefit:

- As has been discussed earlier in this chapter, knowing beforehand the resources that are available for students in your institution, and how access can be made to them, is most helpful, and gives you, as tutor, more confidence in your referral.
- When considering referral, checking with the student whether or not they have seen anyone else about the issue, and how they might feel about talking to someone else, can enable the student to consider this as a useful option to them.
- By explaining what resources are available and how perhaps they could be helpful, you might enable a student to take the first step more readily.
- Exploring with the student what would help them to go to someone else might again enable them to seek the appropriate support. Looking at a relevant leaflet together might be encouraging, and reduce fear of the unknown.
- Explaining why you are suggesting that they see someone else,

being honest about the limits of your expertise, is an important way to help your tutee to realise that you are not trying to 'get rid of them', but are trying to help them to get the support they need. You may suggest that they could come back to tell you what happened, and thus continue to support them as long as necessary.

● Be aware of confidentiality: if you feel it necessary to share with another any information that the student has told you as their tutor, make that clear to the student, and agree together what information you will release, to whom, and how.

● **Finally, any referral is far more likely to be successful from the student's viewpoint, and will encourage independence, if you as tutor give them the tools to self-refer, rather than try to be helpful and do it for them.**

Being a personal tutor can sometimes seem like just another burden on a busy academic, and finding time for tutorials may seem almost impossible. But it can also offer the opportunity to relate to students in a different way. It is a relationship which does not exist in a vacuum, and the significance of the institutional context cannot be underestimated. It is the institution's responsibility to provide the wider support systems upon which both tutor and tutee can draw. Knowing what these are, what they offer and how they can be accessed is a necessary part of the tutor's role. Being able to refer a tutee to these wider support systems appropriately and effectively is a skill which enables tutors to use their knowledge of them for mutual benefit.

Practical suggestions

☐ Remember that, as a personal tutor, you are not the only source of support for students.

☐ Knowing what other areas of support are available, and how what they offer can be accessed, will help you to retain a sense of being part of a wider support system, and not alone in this task.

☐ Be aware that each of the range of support services has its own area of expertise to offer.

☐ Find out which of the support services offer workshops to

staff, especially tutors. These could provide opportunities for your own continuing professional development.

☐ Referring tutees on to further support services is a sign of an effective tutor.

☐ Developing communication with the other support services facilitates appropriate referral.

☐ Recognising when to refer a student, and how to do so successfully are essential skills for an effective tutor.

● **Further reading**

Bell, E. (1996), *Counselling in Further and Higher Education* (Buckingham: Open University Press).

De Board, R. (1998), *Counselling for Toads* (London: Routledge).

Hewitt, E. and Wheeler, S. (2004), 'Counselling in Higher Education: the Experience of the Lone Counsellor', *British Journal of Guidance and Counselling*, 32:4, pp. 533–45.

Lago, C. and Shipton, G. (1994), *Personal Tutoring in Action* (Sheffield: University Counselling Service).

Lees, J. and Vaspe, A. (1999), *Clinical Counselling in Further and Higher Education* (London: Routledge).

Wheeler, S. and Birtle, J. (1993), *A Handbook for Personal Tutors* (Buckingham: Open University Press).

Part Four

Theory into Practice

8 Personal Tutoring for Postgraduate Students

Richard Price

> Parts I to III of the book have looked at a wide range of issues for personal tutors and their tutees in higher education. This chapter aims to explore the subject in relation to postgraduate students.

● Introduction

I am a medical doctor. I qualified in 1986 and progressed to being a full-time partner in General Practice. In 1995 I took up a lecturer's post in the medical school at Newcastle. As part of that role I had responsibility for undergraduate personal tutees.

Since 2001, I have been Course Director for a new course – Graduate Entry to Medicine. This course takes applicants with a previous degree in any subject with a classification of at least a 2.1. They undertake their medical training in four years instead of the conventional five.

Our students have a wide diversity of age, previous background and ethnicity. They also vary in how long it is since they have previously been involved in a course of study, from having finished their degree the year previously to having been away from study for a considerable time, sometimes many years. We have a roughly equal gender mix. Therefore, through this role I have had considerable exposure to the particular challenges of personal tutoring that this group of students bring.

What follows is an overview of this topic based on my own experiences. It includes suggestions (they are no more than that) based on what I have learnt and have found helpful in my tutoring. I have made some literature references, but there is actually very little written on this particular subject. I have also sought the views of my own students.

Any discussion of this nature needs to begin with a definition of the group we are considering. The main type of student we are referring to will be those who have completed one degree and are now engaged in a further academic or vocational course of study. This may be either an extension of, or different from, their original course. However, this definition should also be extended to include those students who have perhaps come to begin their studies at a significantly older age than would conventionally be the case.

● Student issues

As part of the research for this chapter, I conducted a small questionnaire survey of my students to ask them their perceptions of personal tutoring, particularly in so far as they differ (or not) from their thoughts about that role for them as undergraduates. The following is a summary of issues high-lighted by them (in no particular order of prevalence or priority):

- Some felt that they had a greater need of pastoral support than they did as undergraduates.
- Some suggested a need for more help with focusing on career choices.
- Some described a need for their personal tutor to have the ability to know when and where to refer for other types of help.
- They saw their tutor as having an important role as a 'yardstick' to help judge their achievement.
- The qualities they identified as important were to be amiable, knowledgeable, supportive and approachable, and to have a listen-ing, compassionate and understanding ear.
- Many described requiring a less paternalistic relationship, with more of a sense of an equal partnership. Having said this, there was one statement about still needing positive feedback for motivation, suggesting perhaps a mixture of needs in this area (see below).
- There was a need for the tutor to have an ability to give practical advice and support
- Other statements included wanting less guidance as to what to do, and more flexibility and understanding of individuals and their situ-ations and circumstances. They wanted appreciation of, and respect for, their previous education, life experience etc.
- The tutor needed to be able to act as the student's advocate.

Clearly, some of these points are common to all personal tutees. Others, I would suggest, are generally likely to be more characteristic of this particular group of students. I would like to take these points and to look at them in more detail by expanding the issues using my own experiences.

First, it is my experience that these students often suffer considerable stress. Although some of the typical stresses for this group of students will be similar to those for undergraduates, many of the factors that cause them stress will be different from those for undergraduates. I have recently conducted a review of all Graduate Entry to Medicine courses, and virtually all course directors agreed with this point.

As noted above, one issue identified by this small student review was that they felt that they needed *more* pastoral support than when they had been undergraduates.

From my observations and discussions, stressors include (in no particular order of prevalence or priority):

- Much more is riding on the outcome of their learning.
- There is a 'sense of urgency' about learning.
- Most postgraduate training shares a common theme of the self-directed nature of the educational experience. This puts in many ways a much heavier burden on the learner. 'What exactly do I need to know?' 'Where do I go for the information?' 'What will the assessment process comprise?'
- Financial issues.
- Maintaining a 'serious relationship', sometimes with the added factor of this being, at least in part, a long-distance relationship.
- Family commitments.
- Uprooting from an established life.
- Entering a new life with its change of roles, self-identity etc. In my experience this can be a particularly significant source of stress. My guess is that this is because it is something that catches the student by surprise. I think also that this is because sometimes there is the unleashing of a quite profound growth of self-awareness, and many students are frightened or even fearful of what they begin to discover about themselves. The student may be forced by the changes in their life to confront issues which they had perhaps been avoiding or had managed to keep below the 'surface', because suddenly this is no longer possible.
- Peer pressure from other friends who are perceived as being 'further on' with their lives.
- Higher personal expectations of themselves.

The self-directed nature of the learning, coupled with the greater urgency and career relevance of what is being learnt, are a particularly potent stress mix.

Contained within here, also, is another common and self-evident point – that different students will have different needs, and more relevantly, they will wish us to deal with those needs in different ways. There is therefore the generic challenge to us of maintaining a flexible approach, and the need to develop skills in discerning how the student wishes to be helped. Clearly, contained within this statement of the obvious are a number of challenges for us.

● Issues for tutors

I have generated the following based on my own experiences, and on talking to colleagues about theirs. Once again, a number of these challenges are generic to all areas of personal tutoring, but those that are common do have perhaps a different emphasis in the postgraduate arena.

Role definition

This has already been touched upon above. In my experience, this is one of the most important aspects of being a personal tutor, and one of the most difficult things to be clear about.

Gidman, in a literature review of the role of the personal tutor in nursing education, highlights three roles contained within that of the personal tutor – a clinical role, an academic role and a pastoral role (Gidman, 2001). Perhaps we can reasonably expand the 'clinical' role to generalise it to the 'practical and professional' role – one that will often be particularly important in postgraduate settings. As previously stated, this book is concentrating on the personal tutor as a pastoral support to the student.

However, in reality, the implicit role definition of the personal tutor is, by its very nature, often blurred and all-encompassing. This is probably as it should be, given that personal tutors often see their role as being to support students in a wide variety of ways (Rhodes and Jinks, 2005).

Obviously a problem here is that any categorisation of this nature is inherently philosophical, and that in reality these rather abstract categories overlap. The issue then also becomes the allied one of *boundaries* (see below).

Boundaries

Under this heading come issues about the boundaries of how much time you have, how available you want/you are able to be, what is to be discussed, what you are able to help with (and therefore what you are not able to help with). Comfort with this obviously relates to issues discussed earlier, such as awareness of limitations and awareness of who else can help. Into this category also falls the difficult issue of when and how to be contacted. What phone numbers and emails are you going to make available to your tutees, and why? These issues may be more difficult when your relationship with the student is more adult-to-adult, and therefore more equal, and also when perhaps you are more easily able to empathise with the difficulties a particular student may be facing.

This issue can easily be exacerbated by other factors that may blur the boundaries even further. Do you have an academic responsibility for this tutee, and therefore is there potential for conflict between your roles? (See below.) Do you have other or previous skills in the arenas in which help is needed, for example counselling, medical, nursing or mental health training? If so, to what extent, if any, could or should you be using these? There are reports in the literature of nursing tutors seeing their role as analogous to their professional nursing role (Rhodes and Jinks, 2005). To what extent are you going to use these skills? Are there any potential dangers for you in using these skills in a tutoring context? (I, as a GP, often fall into the trap of dealing with the student as if I were their GP. Inevitably, this then leads to all sorts of difficulties, particularly around the theme of boundaries.)

Once again, of course, the easy abstract conclusion is that we should be clear about these boundaries, and apply them fairly and firmly. The reality, as we know, is that often this is impractical, or at least extremely difficult.

Conflict of responsibilities

This relates back to my earlier comments about defining the role. Are there potential conflicts of responsibility and role for you? This is a common theme in the literature relating to personal tutoring (Rhodes and Jinks, 2005; Hart, 1996). Does it have perhaps even greater potential to arise within postgraduate settings? Does the more equal relationship give rise to other potential roles that may conflict, such as those of friend, or mutual support?

An obvious example might be tutoring students for whom you also have some assessment responsibility. Perhaps a more difficult and more common example is treading the line between the advocacy role of wishing to support the student as an individual, versus your faculty responsibility of ensuring that a student is fit to continue their studies.

Developing a relationship

This, of course, is an issue common to all personal tutoring, but perhaps in a postgraduate academic environment, based more around autonomy and independent study, it is potentially more significant. It is a paradox that the personal tutor may be someone that the student knows least well (particularly if roles are separated as above). This, in my experience, is a common problem, and often leads to an exacerbation of the problems noted above. Academic tutors become embroiled in discussions and responsibilities they would rather not have, as a result of statements from students such as 'I just feel I know you much better than my designated personal tutor. This of course appeals powerfully to our desire to help and our liking of being needed!

Time and timings

This I think can be quite tricky to get right, particularly with graduate students. Every academic year it seems that I have tutees who don't want to meet, and who consider regular timetabled meetings with someone whose role is pastoral as a waste of their valuable time. Yet every year it also seems as if I have feedback from other students expressing regret that there aren't more timetabled meetings. Perhaps this central issue here again is that of role definition: What are we for? What are we not for? Close inspection of comments from those students who want more meetings suggests that what they actually seem to want is more of the academic and professional/practical tutoring.

Nevertheless, I'm sure we can all think of students who have decided, for whatever reason, not to say anything about their personal predicaments until such time as those predicaments have produced some degree of destruction of their learning. Students also vary in how insightful they are about pastoral issues that they face, and often, in my experience, those who least welcome such support are those who most need it.

Dealing with your own uncertainty/confidence

It may be that in tutoring graduates you end up with tutees who are the same or a similar age to you, or even older! Furthermore they may be very well qualified, maybe even more qualified than you! Perhaps, however, by being aware of some of the issues previously discussed, this is in reality a difficulty that is quite easy to negotiate.

Support

What are your needs? What extra training do you need? What extra backup and support exists to help you? Who can you talk to about your concerns, or in order to simply 'get it off your chest'?

Clearly there is a lot of overlap with the basic qualities of personal tutors and their approach to undergraduate students, and we obviously should not lose sight of that fact. Some of these fundamental challenges of communication in personal tutoring of postgraduate students are usefully explored through the transactional analysis model. Many of you will be familiar with this model, but for those who are not I include a brief and simplistic overview here.

● Transactional analysis (Berne, 1973)

The transactional model proposes that in any one-to-one discussion each person can be in one of three 'ego states'. Any individual can shift from one state to another.

- *Parent* – the person is in the same state of mind as their parent (Berne, 1973, p. 24). In practice this may be a 'dominant' 'parental' role, perhaps controlling the conversation and the outcomes. This may amount to suggesting, or even telling someone what to do in order to solve a problem.
- *Adult* – the person is in a role of objective reality (Berne, 1973, p. 24). In reality the person is an equal partner in the dialogue, contributing his/her points and listening and responding to the points made by the other.
- *Child* – the person is reacting as they would have when they were a child (Berne, 1973, p. 24). In practice, the person is in a 'passive' mode where s/he has little or no control over the content or outcome of the conversation. The person may wish to be guided or even told what to do to solve a problem.

Essentially, communication between two people continues successfully as long as the roles of both are complementary (Berne, 1973, p. 29). For example, most conversation takes place with both participants in an adult role, listening and modulating what they say as they take into account the contributions of the other. Another example might be if one person is happy to be in a more dominant 'parent' role and the other is happy to be in the more passive 'child' role. However, if the roles are not complementary then the transaction becomes crossed and communication is broken (Berne, 1973, p. 30). An example of this might be:

Tutor: *Have you perhaps thought about changing your accommodation?*

An 'adult' response from the student might be: *No I hadn't. It's perhaps worth a thought,* or *I have, and I don't think it's a good idea because all my friends are close by at the moment.*

A 'child' response, however, might be: *Why do people keep trying to tell me what to do?!,* or *If that's what you think I should do, then I'll do it.*

In this situation, there are two ways for communication to be re-established. One is for the first speaker to change their role to that of 'parent' to complement the 'child'. The other is for the second speaker's 'adult' to be reactivated as a complement to the first speaker's 'adult' (Berne, 1973, p. 31).

It might therefore be possible for us, as tutors, to use an awareness of this to guide students towards a role that maintains communication between us and the student, and enhances rapport. We can usefully apply this simple model to interactions with our tutees.

Postgraduate students in particular will usually wish to remain in 'adult' mode in their dealings with us (see points above). However, sometimes, particularly, in my experience, at times of ill health and emotional crisis, the student will indicate their need for us to take a more 'parent' role, at least temporarily (see points above). This can sometimes be a surprise to us as tutors, when our expectation is of a more adult-to-adult interaction.

Furthermore, there may be examples where a student wishes to retain the passive dependent 'child' role, but we judge it appropriate to encourage the student to take more responsibility and enter the 'adult' role (although we might not necessarily be right!). Therefore we can ask ourselves during conversations with tutees: 'Which of the three roles is each of us in at present?'

To what extent is the student determining or negotiating the agenda, or solutions, and to what extent are they passive or seeming to wish you to take the lead? Following on from this, to what extent is their chosen 'state' appropriate for this particular situation?

In my experience, this is a particularly useful technique when you sense some personal discomfort in the dynamic between you and the student, as it is likely that there is a crossing of roles between you and the student. For example, at times of significant crisis it is entirely reasonable that the student is in 'child' mode. However, there will come a time in their 'recovery' when that is likely to be no longer appropriate. This may result in some discomfort in the interaction, resulting in a 'crossing' of roles. At that point, it may be worth considering the need to utilise phrases that help clarify who is in which role, and that may have the effect of ushering them into the 'adult' state. Some useful questions might be open questions such as:

- What are the issues for you at present?
- How do you see this situation developing?
- What are your thoughts about what could be done about this?

Another variant of this, particularly in our consumerist age, is the student who opt themselves for parent mode, by telling you what to do or demanding of you certain actions. Again, dealing with this begins with recognition. Language to move the student to 'adult' mode can then be used:

I see. Could you explain to me why you would like me to do this?

The particular temptation in these situations may be for us to move directly ourselves into 'parent' mode, and thus put the student immediately into 'child' mode – not a recipe for a successful interview!

I want you to sort my accommodation problems out.

'I think that's up to you to sort!'

(NB: the above is a very simplistic (perhaps too simplistic!) overview of this topic. For a more detailed description please refer to the book *'Games People Play'* by Eric Berne – full reference below.)

To illustrate some of these issues, there follows a case study. The study is based on a real student, though the names, ages etc. have been changed, and some other facts fictionalised, to preserve the anonymity of the student involved.

Samantha was a 28-year-old student, studying on the Graduate Entry to Medicine degree programme. She had done extremely well in her previous degree, having obtained a first class degree in a science allied to medicine. Subsequent to that she had worked for a number of years in the research laboratory of a pharmaceutical company.

She was by nature rather shy, although she had a keen sense of humour, and contributed well in small study groups. She was very knowledgeable, and she had a very conscientious, almost perfectionist nature. She took any work assignment, particularly any work she had to do on behalf of the group, very seriously. About half way through the academic year, she began to develop apparent problems. She found it impossible to speak in her small study group (at which most of the formal teaching took place), and she occasionally had to leave her small group in the middle of sessions. The second time this happened, her group tutor (who was not her personal tutor) approached Samantha and asked if she could have a chat with her.

What would you have said to Samantha at this point?
What would you have done next?

At that meeting, her tutor gently began probing as to what it was that was upsetting Samantha. She carefully and repeatedly emphasised that her prime focus was to help, not to judge or punish in any way.

Samantha volunteered that about a year previously her father had died suddenly at the age of 53. At the time she had been very busy with a prestigious project at work, and therefore had not properly gone through the grieving process, but had pushed her emotions to one side. That situation had been exacerbated by her having to give a lot of emotional support to her mother. For some reason, however, she was now beginning to ruminate a lot about her father's death. This was causing her severe emotional upset.

The tutor asked for permission to speak to her personal tutor, and suggested that Samantha do the same as soon as possible.

If you were Samantha's personal tutor, how would you respond to the conversation with your colleague?

Samantha's tutor emailed Samantha and asked her to contact him to arrange a time to meet.

He began the meeting by asking Samantha to describe what had been happening, keeping the questions as open as possible initially, and being aware of his non-verbal communication in encouraging her to feel safe and to talk. He then probed more deeply, in order to get an understanding as to how this situation was affecting her studies.

He ascertained that Samantha was struggling to concentrate, and was finding it particularly difficult to contribute in group situations. The workload was such, however, that she was then becoming extremely anxious about falling behind, and was thus compensating by working into the small hours of the morning every day.

He discussed with her various options for her studies; these included a short leave of absence, or a postponement of her studies for a year. However, as it was the end of term, they decided to see how things were after the 2-week Easter holidays.

He also offered to explore the possibilities of her getting an extension to the submission deadline for a major course assignment, and suggested she submit a form for extenuating circumstances to be considered in the event of examination failure.

The complicating factor for the tutor was that he was also a practising GP. After the initial discussion, he began to ask her about medical symptoms, as he was keen to try to establish whether Samantha had a depressive illness that might be amenable to treatment. As part of his medical assessment of a patient with such symptoms, he also specifically asked Samantha if she had had any thoughts about harming herself. After a long silence Samantha tearfully admitted to having had quite serious thoughts of harming herself. The tutor was alarmed and suggested she consult her own GP as soon as possible. He arranged to see her again himself the next day. He gave her his home and mobile phone numbers, and also phoned her that evening just to check she was OK.

After the meeting he was aware that perhaps he had crossed boundaries. He felt uncomfortable that he had not clarified the official faculty approach to managing such situations, and also felt considerable anxiety about Samantha's mental state and what she might do. He therefore rang and spoke to a senior faculty member who was a close friend, about the encounter (without mentioning Samantha's name).

What do you think about how this tutor handled the situation? What would you have done the same/ differently?

The following day Sam was much the same, and had not yet arranged to see her doctor. The tutor urged her to do so, but he remained very anxious. He arranged to telephone her every day and reiterated the advice he gave her the previous day to phone him if there was a crisis.

Three days later, he got a call on his mobile at 7.30 p.m. from Samantha's best friend. Samantha had taken an overdose and was at that moment just leaving the casualty department. She had asked her friend to phone the tutor as she wanted to know if she could see him the next day 'to discuss things'.

What is your emotional reaction to this request?
How would you respond?

The tutor asked to speak directly to Sam. He agreed to see her the next day, but stated that it was important that she make an appointment with her GP as soon as possible in order to sort out the medical issues. He emphasised that he could not take any medical responsibility for her, and that his role was to focus on supporting her academically.

At that meeting, the tutor managed to resist the temptation to ask about medical factors, although he did clarify that Sam was no longer actively suicidal. He focussed the discussion on how the situation should be managed with regard to Sam's studies. He reiterated the various options as before, and re-emphasised that the priority for the faculty was to support her in any way they could.

He once more discussed with Sam the need for her to be followed up by her GP, clarifying the boundary of his responsibilities by stating emphatically that it was in neither her best interests nor his that he take any medical responsibility for her. He apologised to her for having done that so far. He suggested that should there be a medical crisis she should contact her local GP or casualty department, or ring the Samaritans.

He also fulfilled his obligation to the faculty by explaining gently that the faculty would need medical certification of her fitness to progress into the next year of her studies.

How do you feel about how the tutor has managed this contact? What would you do next?

The tutor arranged to continue to see Samantha on a weekly basis initially. At those meetings, he concentrated firmly on the issues related to her study, and continued to emphasise the importance for Samantha of having regular follow up with her GP. He also discussed things with the head of the faculty personal tutoring system, with Samantha's permission, and he discussed the situation with the Head of Faculty, and on one occasion they conducted a joint consultation with Sam, again with her permission.

Over the next weeks, Samantha gradually improved. The tutor scaled down the frequency of their meetings. She passed the year with flying colours.

This 'case' highlights a number of the issues referred to above:

- The failure of the tutor to establish boundaries and to 'contract' with the student. This was finally done, but it was far more awkward when done later, and the tutor had the sense of 'pushing the student away' at the time when she was most vulnerable.
- The tutor allowed himself to take on too much responsibility, (largely, in this case, because the tutor was also a GP and took on that role).
- He failed to refer appropriately to senior members of faculty who had more direct responsibility for more serious and difficult personal tutoring issues. This led to much more stress for him, but may have also left him more vulnerable to censure from the faculty had things gone badly wrong.
- He did, however, discuss his conversations with a trusted senior colleague. This helped him cope with the stress of the situation.
- He had to negotiate his role with Samantha between being supportive and facilitatory, but also as a course 'policeman' by requesting the report for progression.
- There were some transactional conflicts at times during this story, which the tutor was slow to address because it did not fit in with his expectations. During the worst phases of Samantha's problems, she naturally displayed the 'child' mode. However, this persisted, and was evidenced by:
  - not making an appointment for follow up with the GP despite being asked to do so by the tutor;
  - passive language and body language during the meetings.

- However, inadvertently the tutor encouraged this imbalance by the 'parent' mode he chose to adopt – contacting her daily, etc. It may be that he was wrong to expect her to behave in a more 'adult' way. However, he could have explored this issue in greater depth.

Summary

- Although there is much overlap between personal tutoring issues for undergraduate and postgraduate students, there are a number that are likely to be different.
- Many of the stresses experienced by postgraduate students are perhaps more likely to be stressors that we, as fellow adults, naturally empathise with.
- There is more potential for confusion about role definition and the nature of the relationship between student and tutee. This requires awareness and an ability to be flexible in approach.

Practical suggestions

☐ Consider the need as a personal tutor to develop skills to promote the tutee's ability to reflectively appraise their own performance, strengths and weaknesses.

☐ Develop the ability to define your role, and help set the agenda, in consultation with students. Consider your need to develop skills that enable you to set the boundaries for what you will be able, and not able, to do.

☐ Establish clear lines of communication between yourselves as personal tutors and academic tutors, where necessary. Decide clearly which of these two roles retains responsibility for the third of my listed roles where it exists – the professional and practical tutor. Ensure that both you and the student are familiar with the established systems of responsibility, referral and backup in your institution. As an important addition to this, aspects of confidentiality need to be clarified.

☐ Take care to avoid the temptation to regard the stresses experienced by postgraduate students as *greater*, perhaps because they are the sorts of stressors to which we as adults can more easily relate. It is inappropriate to make such value judgements, one way or another.

☐ Be aware of how your training in other areas might impinge on the tutor – student relationship.

☐ Consider using the transactional model in one-to-one discussions with tutees. Ask yourself 'What mode am I in?' 'What mode is the student in?' (particularly if you have a sense of discomfort in the meeting).

☐ Take every opportunity to get to know your tutees informally. In many ways the maturity of the student often lends itself to making it easier to establish a relationship, as that relationship may have a more equal balance.

☐ Consider scheduling regular meetings and making these compulsory. If all is well the meeting needn't take too long. Even if nothing is discussed, it is an opportunity to build the relationship.

☐ Try to develop awareness of your own limitations. Be clear about which of your limitations you are happy to accept, and which you need to address.

☐ Know where to turn for help for yourself, in terms of both training and support. Don't be shy in talking to someone.

● **Further reading**

Berne, E. (1973), *Games People Play*, 4th edition (New York: Ballantine Books).

9 Suggested Model of Best Practice for Personal Tutoring

Lindsey Neville

This chapter will present and discuss a model of personal tutoring developed in response to research findings at the University of Worcester.

● Personal tutoring model of care

Addressing the needs of both staff and students requires a robust approach to the care which post-1992 higher education demands of its personal tutoring. This approach needs to be reliable and resilient and to offer appropriate regard to all involved. A personal tutoring model, 'The 3 Rs of Care' (Figure 9.1), combines all three of these factors. It offers the opportunity for early intervention through the development of positive relationships between personal tutors and their tutees. These positive relationships may reap rewards for both parties. It takes the view that, just as suggested by Taylor (2006), our view of academic life can be complemented by someone whose view may be slightly more pragmatic than our own.

This model of care reinforces the cyclical nature of the work, in that rather than offering solutions it offers opportunities for further exploration and discovery. Egan (1990) suggests that 'actions are heuristic; they can find more problems, they can uncover blind spots, they can help set priorities' (p. 179). Therefore actions suggested or undertaken seek to '*generate more of the story*' (p. 179). The more actions that we take to improve the care that we offer within the academic community the greater will be our access to more detail of the story. Consequently, actions identified are not goals in themselves but ways of moving towards an ever-changing model of best practice.

The positive relationships that this model can generate will provide a firm foundation for intervention throughout the duration of the course. A system that links this development of constructive relationships with the curriculum will offer further opportunities for tutors to have an impact on a wide range of issues that influence student learning and retention, and enhance the reliability of the relationship. A reliable personal tutoring system will ensure that student requests are met at the point of need. Individual tutors will have their own ideas and thoughts on how these elements of a successful personal

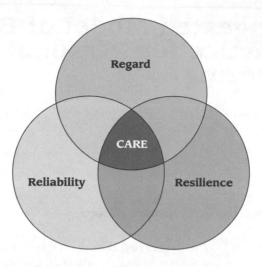

Figure 9.1   The three Rs of care: a personal tutoring model

tutoring relationship can best be demonstrated, but some of the key elements are presented here.

Tutoring relationships need to be underpinned by support for those who deliver the front line care. This support is effective when provided mutually by colleagues, but to provide resilience it needs to be endorsed by institutions and validated by a system which provides accessibility for all. This will also ensure opportunities for the dissemination of ideas that will lead to raising the profile of the discipline.

● Reliability

The role of the personal tutor is highly regarded by staff and students alike. It is viewed by almost everyone as having a fundamental part to play in a successful student support system. Student narratives demonstrate that the provision of a reliable personal tutorial system makes a vital contribution to student retention, with many students attributing their continued presence on the course to the support of their tutor. One student told me 'I might have given up if it hadn't been for my tutor's encouragement and support.' Her experience is typical of students whose stories evidence the importance of the assistance that they have received from their tutor.

There appear to be a number of key features of a reliable system. These features include ensuring that students have access to appropriate support at the point of need; the use of a consistent personal tutoring model; acknowledging specific needs of part-time staff and students; and ensuring ease of access through efficient communication systems.

Access to support at the point of need

It is important to establish a means of support at the point of need. Given the flexible nature of working in higher education, staff may not be available as quickly as students would have liked. For example, Gail 'left university feeling upset about what had happened and wishing that she could have talked to someone then and there'. There are a number of support systems within institutions that could have provided alternative support but students viewed these as remote, as they 'wouldn't have wanted to talk to a stranger'. Students appear reluctant to use support services that involve staff who are unfamiliar to them.

It is debatable whether any student support service can provide the immediate support that student circumstances sometimes require. Although the personal tutor system should not be viewed as an emergency service there are clearly occasions when student support needs necessitate a prompt response. There were considerable differences in experiences of gaining this type of support. Many students felt able to access support promptly but others highlighted considerable delays in eliciting a response. A more robust approach to meeting urgent need would ensure that help-seeking behaviour of distressed students (University of Leicester, 2002) is recognised and addressed and the safety net around students enlarged (Stanley and Manthorpe, 2002).

Students felt that there was no clear point of contact within their departments when information or support was needed quickly. They found themselves wandering round the building 'hoping to bump into someone who might help them'. Tutors were viewed as the primary source of help. Many students did not know who the course administrator was and there was little recognition of the role that administrative staff might play in signposting or providing information. Staff stories evidenced a high dependence on the wealth of information and skills that they hold, but it appears that students felt that this source of support was inaccessible to them.

Consistent personal tutoring model

For over a quarter of the staff respondents the number of different models used for personal tutoring affected the reliability of the system. Additionally the lack of consistency in the allocation of personal tutees created problems for some personal tutors. Several personal tutors had tutees from three different personal tutoring models. It was felt that tutor groups which mixed students from different models were disadvantageous as the differing demands created uncertainty and confusion for the personal tutor: 'I need to remember different protocols, different processes, different paperwork and different deadlines.' These add to the time commitment required to support the student effectively. Use of a consistent tutoring model is therefore seen as beneficial to the level of support that a tutor is able to give. There did seem to be some benefits from meetings of mixed groups, where tutors see their students as a whole group, as it can result in a wider circle of acquaintances, which may assist integration in the early stages of university life – my tutor arranged several "information" sessions in the first semester that gave me the opportunity to meet other first years, it really widened my circle of familiar faces at a time when everything was so strange'.

Students expressed a preference for a curriculum model of personal tutoring. They felt that they had made early attachments to module tutors, who are largely perceived as empathic and caring. When they discussed periods of difficulty that they had experienced it was often a module tutor that they confided in: 'I eventually confided in a module tutor who was very understanding and helpful.'

One of the common criticisms of students was the lack of consistency in the information given by tutors, this related largely to the role of personal development planning (PDP) in tutorials. Many still referred to it as the Student Qualities Profile (SQP) and there was confusion, on the part of both staff and students, about the part that the PDP plays in the relationship between tutor and tutee. Others, particularly those students in the 25+ age range, were particularly critical of the emphasis that their personal tutors placed on the PDP.

Insights

My personal tutor told me that personal tutorials were entirely focused on Personal Development Planning. It took me a long time to work out what it actually was. I then didn't think that it was relevant to me as a mature student so I made no further attempts to contact my personal tutor and he has never contacted me. So I suppose it's not all that important really?

One student told me that her personal tutor 'has never mentioned PDP'. This lack of consistency on the role of PDP was apparent throughout the research. 'She didn't seem to know what she was talking about' is representative of the range of comments received by a group of students who appeared disaffected and for whom the personal tutor system was not viewed as a credible source of support.

Communication

Methods of communication between personal tutors and tutees affect availability and this in turn affects the reliability of the system. From the student perspective, staff availability appears inconsistent with their needs. 'It took me four weeks to get a tutorial with my personal tutor' was representative of a number of comments from students. Others were very positive about their experiences: 'She made me feel that I mattered. I can't thank her enough.' The range of experiences underlines the individuality of that experience.

Where both the tutor and the student are part-time an additional strain is placed on the reliability of the system and exacerbates the problems of effective communication.

Insights

One of my own personal students is part-time, and so am I; I am also her independent study tutor. It is so difficult for us to make plans to meet, creating what seems to be an unnecessary strain on our relationship.

Students recognised and appreciated that lectures were often concentrated into three days of the week. However, although this timetabling appears to be intended to provide the student with flexibility, the consequence is that their attendance days are often filled with academic commitments, leaving little flexibility for personal tutorials. Students are using their non- attendance days for their employment and caring responsibilities. This means that demands made on student time while on campus are wideranging and require efficient organisation and time management on the part of the student. Many students are putting personal tutorials low down on their priorities until the point of immediate need. This again highlights the importance of forming positive relationships early on in the course as a means of investing for the future. Given the accepted importance of this first year of study in student retention (Rickinson and Rutherford, 1995) and the number of personal tutors consulted by students prior to withdrawal from the course (Rickinson and Rutherford, 1995; University College Worcester, 2003), there is a need to raise the profile of this important first contact with staff.

Concern was expressed about the difficulty of making tutorial arrangements. A variety of methods was used including telephone, email and booking through a timetable system on the door. Students felt that staff were often poor at responding to both telephone calls and emails. The email system was perceived as particularly problematic by both tutors and tutees.

'She never replies to my emails – I have given up,' reflects a level of frustration that was evident in much of the communication between staff and students. Students often spoke of email as being their preferred method of contact with staff. It is seen as being quick, easy and direct. This technique of tutoring is achieved relatively easily but is clearly effective in sending positive messages to students.

Although for many students the availability of their personal tutor was a matter for concern, personal tutors' view of how available they make themselves was coloured by frequent experiences of students who book tutorials and then don't turn up. One tutor 'had 6 students in one week who failed to turn up for pre-booked appointments.' This may have an impact on staff willingness to make themselves fully available.

To maintain the reliability of the personal tutoring system it is important for individual tutors to consider which method of contact works best for them and their students. This then needs to be communicated to tutees so that all are clear about the tutor's preferred method of contact.

● Regard

Rogers (1967) puts at the centre of a helping relationship a respect, which he describes as 'unconditional positive regard' (p. 102). This involves communicating to the client, or in this case, the student, genuine concern that is unaffected by personal judgements. Therefore, for the purposes of this discussion, regard is viewed as the quality of those interactions between tutor and tutee. This quality is affected by the nature of the initial contact and the student's perception of how approachable the tutor is.

Initial contact

The first meeting with tutors is viewed by students as vital in determining the subsequent value of the personal tutor. Students' descriptions of the first contact with their tutor evidenced diverse experiences of this initial contact. Where these early experiences had been positive a firm foundation was secured for the future.

Barriers to the development of these affirmative relationships were wide ranging. Where positive relationships had not formed it was viewed as the responsibility of the staff, who students perceived as too busy or uninterested. There were examples of breakdown in relationships; these invariably resulted in lost opportunities for the students, who were generally unaware that it was possible to change personal tutor. The response to these problems was an avoidance of all contact, which resulted in a lack of opportunity for intervention when troubles occurred later in the course. One student provides an example of this in that she felt unable to contact her tutor when problems emerged because an early relationship had not been established.

Insights

As a result of my experiences I became very withdrawn from the course and contemplated leaving but felt unable to contact my personal tutor as earlier approaches had been met with little warmth or interest.

Where this first encounter was negative or did not take place, students felt abandoned and without a point of reference. This early contact appears to be very significant for students – one student told me that her tutor had never contacted her 'so I didn't bother either'. There were other examples of negative first experiences, largely related to induction opportunities for personal tutees. Several students identified this lack of contact at induction as defining in terms of their relationship with their personal tutor. One student described it as rejection: 'those of us whose personal tutors couldn't be bothered to turn up were just left to one side'.

The positive power of these early contacts was also demonstrated by students who felt supported from the first meeting: 'from the very beginning I knew she was someone that I would go to if I needed someone to talk to'.

Interpersonal skills

Many of the case studies evidenced high-level interpersonal skills on the part of the personal tutor. Where personal tutors are successful in developing positive relationships with their personal tutees it allows them to have an impact on a wide range of complex academic and social issues. These tutors are trusted and valued and there are significant examples of the difference they make to their tutees lives, as in the case of one student who told me that 'I don't think I could have kept going without her'. The enthusiasm, interpersonal skills and aptitude of those entrusted with the role are paramount in securing positive outcomes from the relationship.

'I found her very cold' and 'I felt as if I were of little consequence' were examples of students' experience, that suggest that not all personal tutors are as successful in forming positive relationships with their tutees.

The current method of allocating personal tutees to all academic staff fails to account for their individual capacity to undertake the role. There is an apparent assumption that all lecturing staff are suitable for the role, as job descriptions place little emphasis on the skills necessary to undertake it.

Those who value this aspect of their work are more likely to access appropriate professional development and prioritise personal tutorials in their workload.

There are barriers to these idealised, successful communications between tutors and tutees. The quality of the interaction was sometimes affected by the lack of privacy caused by staff sharing office space. The need to go and find a private space was viewed as highly problematic and unprofessional. The number of staff who identified the problematic nature of sharing office space is likely to be an under-representation, as one of the departments used in the research has a much higher proportion of staff who have their own space.

There were issues of gender, which had an impact on the interactions for both staff and students. A male member of staff told me that one of his students made him feel very uncomfortable.

One of my first year female students is 18. She booked appointments to see me at least once a week in the first semester. At first I thought she was just anxious to get things right and I spent time reassuring her. In the second semester she took two of the modules for which I was module leader. On several occasions she stayed behind after the lecture and I became aware that she was seeking me out far more often than was necessary for her learning. I often found her waiting near my office. I felt at a loss to know how to deal with her attention but was worried where it might lead if I did nothing.

Eventually I confided in my line manager who suggested that she reassign her to another personal tutor. It didn't solve the problem as I was still involved with teaching her but it limited the opportunities for necessary contact. I tried to ensure that I was never alone with her, which made me feel less vulnerable. Gradually the attention she paid to me lessened but it left me feeling very uncertain of my relationship with female students, which I think will affect how I relate to them in the future.

Students in both of the departments used for the research are predominantly female and there was concern from some of the male personal tutors that it was inappropriate for them to be alone with female students. The issue of gender appears to be of greater significance for staff than for students and more significant for male staff than female staff. In order for staff to provide a reliable service to students they need to feel safe and unthreatened by the relationships that they need to form.

The greatest criticism from staff was levied at the absence of designated, allocated and protected time for personal tutorials. Therefore the reliability of the system would be enhanced if the role was prioritised in academic staff workloads.

Diversity

An awareness of cultural diversity is central to the ability to demonstrate appropriate regard to students.

> One of my students came from a strict Hindu background. Her parents came to Britain from Pakistan just before she was born. They were proud of her academic achievement and were pleased that she had gained a place at university. She followed their wishes and enrolled on an undergraduate course at her local university rather than move away from home. She was anxious to please them. I saw her regularly and she seemed to have made a lot of friends and to be flourishing in the university environment. She started going out with a fellow student who was from a white British background. At the beginning of the third year she emailed me and asked to see me urgently. She was very upset and told me that her parents had found out about her relationship. They had made clear to her that they expected her to make an arranged marriage. I spent a long time talking to her and she tried to explain that to disobey her parents would be seen as a huge act of disrespect and might end with her being forced into the marriage. I found it very difficult to reconcile in my own mind the confident student that I had come to know with the one before me who was feeling lonely, confused and desperate for support. I had no experience of arranged marriages and felt that all she needed to do was explain to her parents how unhappy this would make her. I tried to help her by talking through how she might discuss her concerns with her parents, impressing on them her unhappiness. I failed to understand the difficulties posed for her by this clash of her own western lifestyle with her parents deeply held belief system. This lack of understanding obviously came across to her as she stopped confiding in me.

● Resilience

The British Association for Counselling and Psychotherapy (BACP, 2005) identifies resilience as one of the personal moral qualities to which those using counselling skills in a helping context might aspire. The capacity to work with the student's concerns without being personally diminished might similarly be recommended to personal tutors. As a personal tutor I am operating with the same student stories that I worked with as counsellor. There are some differences but they are related more to the process than to the content. This capacity to work with the concerns of others depends upon appropriate training to recognise personal limitations, and the identification of support strategies to manage the potential emotional impact of the work.

Range of issues

The issues that students bring will also have an impact on a tutor's ability to maintain that resilience and 'influence the effectiveness of the help that we offer other people' (Geldard and Geldard, 2003, p. 28). Students had felt it was appropriate to discuss a wide range of issues with personal tutors. There were a considerable number of powerful stories of tutors having an impact on often complex and entrenched social issues. This means that tutors were expected to provide support in a wide range of academic, emotive, and personal development arenas, with very little individual support for the role.

Student and staff data showed consistency in the use made of these personal tutorials. Academic progress, study skills and careers were expected as key issues but both staff and students put stress in the top four issues discussed at tutorials. For some tutors this is an area of work that they feel challenges their resources: 'Several of my students have asked me for help in coping with their stress. I don't know what to do'. However, those students who discussed stress felt that their tutor had been very helpful in aiding them in finding coping strategies for their stress. As stress is a crucial factor in the development of mental health difficulties (University of Leicester, 2002) this aspect of the work with personal tutees has particular significance for maintaining student mental health. The incidence of stress as a part of personal tutorials may account for the increase that the majority (65 per cent) of personal tutors have seen in the level of support that they need to offer tutees. The average number of years' experience of the respondents is eight, which means that the bulk of their experience has been in the period after 1992 when the number of students entering HE increased.

This increase seen by personal tutors in the levels of distress amongst students supports that identified by Easton and Van Laar (1995) and reflects concerns about the increase in poor mental health amongst young people generally (Roberts, 2002). There are therefore implications for the overall impact on staff who are increasingly involved in working with both distressed and mentally ill students. Support for this demanding role comes predominantly from colleagues. These informal discussions with colleagues, as a means of coping with personal tutors' concerns, are highly valued by all staff. This collegiate response is seen as unrecognised and therefore perhaps undervalued. Such informal systems of collaborative support lack both a firm foundation and institutional recognition.

Levels of distress are impacting on the well being of the staff. Freudenberger (1980) cautions against the depletion of personal physical and mental resources in the support of others. The key factors of a difficult environment, demanding clients and poor skills at setting limits on their involvement, which Nelson-Jones (2001) identifies in the emotional exhaustion and burnout of helpers, are evident in the data. One personal tutor described her own 'desire to look after her (the student) and to try to make good the negative experiences in her life'. This caring response to the distress of the student is indicative of the issues that Nelson identifies. As a counsellor working with this student I would have needed to accept that this might be based more on my need to make things right for her than being an appropriate response to her needs.

The ability to impose personal boundaries, which protect self, is a skill associated with counsellor training and overseen by regular professional supervision. However, personal tutors are operating in an environment in which they may become emotionally exhausted by the demands of their students, but are lacking the professional support available to their clinical colleagues. Some of the case studies demonstrated the impact on the tutor where issues discussed by the student touched on issues in their own life ' – 'I was upset for some time afterwards as I felt I had let her down as I struggled to deal with my own grief'.

The counselling service was highly valued by those staff who used it as a means for personal support. However, the support was viewed as a 'last resort' rather than a support system that is integrated into a coherent model of student services provision. The staff using the counselling service as a means of support were in the minority, and staff were generally unaware of it as a source of support for difficult student concerns.

Continuing professional development

In contrast to Easton and Van Laar (1995), this study found that personal tutors were very well qualified for the work. This may be a reflection of its increasing importance through the intervening 10 years as a result of student retention issues connected with widening participation since 1992. It is possible that, given the nature of the two disciplines used in the research (health and early childhood studies), these staff will hold an existing professional qualification prior to entering employment in HE, which may account for the high levels of qualification in counselling skills. There was a general willingness to engage in the work and undertake the necessary training supporting continuing professional development. Despite this level of commitment to professional development, there was a recognition of the need for further development opportunities to meet the developing needs of the role. In house staff development courses in counselling skills were highly valued by those who had attended. Notwithstanding training or further development undertaken, there was a percentage who still felt unprepared for the wide variety of demands placed upon them. Those who had undertaken no specific professional development in relation to personal tutoring were also less likely to feel equipped for the role.

● Institutional responsibilities

The research at the University of Worcester highlights a number of management issues which need addressing to improve the experience of both personal tutors and their students:

- Inconsistent tutoring models create confusion and uncertainty. Students prefer the curriculum model, making early attachments with module tutors.
- One of the most common criticisms of personal tutoring relates to personal development planning. Staff and students are confused about the role that this should play in the relationship between tutor and tutee and there is huge inconsistency in the implementation.
- Effective communication and support are compromised when part-time students are paired with part-time staff.
- Staff stories evidence high dependency on the wealth of information and skills that administrators hold, but students did not seem to know who the administrator was and felt that this source of potential support was inaccessible to them.
- The quality of personal tutoring is very mixed. There are many examples of excellent practice but also examples of what students perceive as rejection. This may be attributable to the lack of designated and protected time for tutorials, which appears incongruous with the importance the part that should be placed on the role of the personal tutor in student retention and that these should play in the relationship between tutor and tutee.
- A central 'body' is needed to oversee the management, the dissemination of information and the development of personal tutoring.
- Tutors have seen an increase in the levels of distress presented by students. This reflects concerns about increased levels of poor mental health amongst young people generally. There are implications for the impact on the health of tutors.
- Support for the role comes largely from colleagues. This collegiate response is seen as unrecognised and undervalued.
- Generally speaking, personal tutors were very well qualified for the work. Many had undertaken additional qualifications in counselling

skills. However, there was still a recognition of the need for further development opportunities to meet the growing needs of the role.

- Tutors are not primarily an emergency service, but it is hard to recognise and accept that sometimes there may be no one available to connect with students in distress in a timely manner. There is therefore a need to ensure a reliable system of fast-tracking support for some students in some circumstances.
- Staff and students can be unaware of who their tutees and tutors are. This appears to be particularly problematic when changes are made throughout the year.
- Robust systems need to be in place to address staff sickness and the impact on tutees.

Establishing the '3 Rs' model of personal tutoring in the face of these difficulties may require institutions to consider a number of short- and long-term measures.

Shorter-term measures

- Where possible, assign year one mandatory module tutors as personal tutors.
- Clarify management expectations with regard to personal development planning.
- Part-time students should be allocated personal tutors who are full-time members of staff.
- Encourage regular contact with tutees through email.
- Administrators could be introduced to students at induction and act as signposts to further information. They have the advantage of (usually) being available.
- Ideally, all students need to be seen by their personal tutors in the first week of the course.
- Encourage sharing of best practice and dissemination of information.
- Raise the profile of personal tutoring as a discipline in its own right through discussion and dissemination of information.
- Promote awareness of the university counselling service as a means of support for staff in their work with students.
- Staff development sessions need to take place immediately prior to the start of the new academic year.
- Publicise widely (to both staff and students) where students who are in distress should go.

- Update personal tutor lists regularly and tell tutors personally if changes are made to their list.

Longer-term measures

- Management policy decisions are needed to establish a core model for tutoring.
- Establish a minimum expectation with staff assigned to students in one scheme only.
- Arrange continuing professional development (CPD) sessions for administrative staff to facilitate an expansion of their role, particularly focusing on referral skills.
- Minimise the number of group emails during semester time so that the emphasis is on communication from students.
- Encourage regular contact with tutees through email.
- Personal tutoring needs to be valued by including it in the workload allocation. This could ultimately be work only undertaken by those with an aptitude and enthusiasm.
- An academic member of staff is needed to take responsibility for leading the way in personal tutoring matters and supporting staff in the role.
- Support for staff needs to be integrated into a coherent model of student services provision.
- Greater emphasis and value should be placed on the existing staff development courses. Encourage staff to attend. There should be more focused advertising of CPD opportunities.
- Induction sessions for both staff and students should include an introduction to all key staff from Student Services.

● Summary

The personal tutor system is highly valued by both staff and students, but there is currently a recognition and concern that the chances of a successful relationship between personal tutor and student 'can be likened to that of winning the lottery'.

Effective personal tutor relationships can be seen as those which develop from the earliest tutorial opportunities. These relationships can then provide a firm foundation for support in the years ahead. They are dependent upon the communication skills of the tutor and the willingness of both the student and the tutor to engage in the process. Students who are able to access appropriate support are often able to resolve or deal with difficult issues.

> - My personal tutor really helped; she listened to how upset I was but also helped me make a plan for how I could still get all my assignments in. I couldn't have managed it without her.
> - From the very beginning I knew she was someone that I would go to if I needed someone to talk to.

Barriers to the development of the relationship mean that opportunities for appropriate intervention in times of need are often lost. It is these initial lost opportunities that create many of the difficulties for students in accessing the support they need. Efficient communication systems between tutor and student are therefore essential for the development of effective relationships. When communication systems fail, students are likely to 'give up'.

These positive interactions need to be underpinned by support for those who deliver the front line care. Colleagues provide the majority of support mutually, but new colleagues may struggle to cope with the demands made on them.

A personal tutoring model which is effective in providing appropriate support to both staff and student, will therefore be one that places reliability, regard and resilience at the core of its care.

Exemplar

Returning to the story of Leanne used in the introduction offers an opportunity to show the value of the understanding offered by this new model of personal tutoring. The student, who described her experiences of distress and the support offered to her, felt 'unable to contact my personal tutor as earlier approaches had been met with little warmth or interest'. She could very easily have become one of the students who withdraw from the course without discussing it with anyone. The key to the importance of appropriate support is highlighted by her own words: 'I eventually confided in a module tutor who was understanding and helpful. She listened and made me feel that it was worth trying to sort things out.'

It was fortunate that this student had formed a positive relationship with one of her module tutors as this gave the opportunity for an intervention that kept her on the course. This intervention gave her the opportunity to both continue with her studies and work through, with the help of a referral to the university counsellor, issues that may otherwise have led to the potential tragic consequences of inadequate support for students discussed by Stanley and Manthorpe (2002). Had the student and tutor developed an early positive relationship it is likely that she would have been able to seek guidance and support at a much earlier stage.

This model of demonstrating care in the academic community seeks to enlarge the safety net around students from the very beginning of the course. This can be achieved if institutions put the personal tutor at the heart of a robust support system that acknowledges the importance of early intervention and underlines the need for supporting both tutors and students.

Practical suggestions

A range of practical suggestions for supporting the 3 Rs model of care in the academic community are presented in Chapter 9.

● **Further reading**

Egan, G. (1990), *Skilled Helper*, 4th edn (London: Wadsworth).
Stanley, N. and Manthorpe, J. (eds) (2002), *Students' Mental Health Needs: Problems and Responses* (London: Jessica Kingsley).

10 The Personal Tutor's Tool Kit

Lindsey Neville

This chapter will explore a range of skills which personal tutors may find useful in their work with students. It considers the importance of support for those undertaking the work, and the value of continuing professional development in equipping academic staff for their role as personal tutors.

● Introduction

The consideration of academic support for students in higher education necessitates an acknowledgement that learners are at different stages of their lives; this is equally relevant for pastoral support. The different life stages of the student will have an impact upon their expectation and use of the tutorial system. Tutors also bring to the mix their own experiences and expectations which will affect the outcome of the tutorial.

Insights

Recently, a new colleague confided in me that he felt out of his depth with the neediness of many of his tutees and the breadth of issues that he was expected to deal with. He felt that he just didn't have sufficient knowledge or experience to ensure that the students had a quality experience of the personal tutor system. I tried to reassure him that enthusiasm and motivation could always be their equal since with knowledge and experience can also come complacency, as I am aware that when I become entrenched in the endless rounds of the academic year I sometimes forget the importance of my role to each individual.

Race (2001) discusses the difficulty in seeing a clear dividing line between academic tutorials and personal tutorials. The reality is that where both of these roles are invested in the same person there is no dividing line. In the modern world of higher education the personal tutor must usually manage both roles alongside each other, making it a task that may inevitably bring conflicts. What I hope to achieve in working with my students is the creation of a safe, ongoing relationship in which the students might express their concerns and ask for help when appropriate. This needs to be achieved without compromising the student's independent learning.

The model of personal tutoring suggested in Chapter 9 requires a combination of three factors: regard, reliability and resilience. To be effective these need to be applied using a variety of practitioner skills, strategies and techniques. Many of the skills of being a personal tutor are closely allied with those of being a counsellor. However, it is important to draw the important distinction between acting as a counsellor and using counselling skills.

Counselling

In recent years the word 'counselling' has become an all-embracing term for anything from a chat with a cup of tea to a formalised relationship with an accredited practitioner. However, the British Association for Counselling and Psychotherapy (BACP, 2006) defines counselling as what

> takes place when a counsellor sees a client in a private and confidential setting to explore a difficulty the client is having, distress they may be experiencing or perhaps their dissatisfaction with life, or loss of a sense of direction and purpose.   (BACP, 2006)

Professional counsellors work within a specific theoretical model, have attended an accredited course of study and have an understanding of both psychology and human development (Geldard and Geldard, 2003). Counsellors work within an ethical framework. The use of counselling in higher education is discussed further in Chapter 7.

Counselling skills

Counselling skills are a set of tools, used in any setting, that enable any user to help others communicate. The use of these skills does not turn the user into a counsellor. They are a way of helping another person to communicate the difficult and often private areas of their lives. Talking about the issues may then help them to perhaps see the situation differently, make a decision or cope with their worries or anxieties.

As a counsellor I can choose when to act as a counsellor and when to use counselling skills. Similarly, personal tutors can choose whether or not they put counselling skills into practice. It may not always be appropriate to utilise the skills, as in the case of a meeting I had with Phil.

Phil came in early to a lecture at which I was expecting 30 students. As we were chatting while waiting for everyone to arrive he started to tell me that he was struggling with an assignment because he had missed some sessions owing to difficulties at home. He was clearly upset and wanted to talk, but students were starting to arrive and so it would not have been appropriate to use counselling skills to help Phil to tell me about the difficulties, as it might have left him vulnerable in front of his peers. I was able to deflect the conversation through the use of closed rather than open questions and then as more students arrived I ended the conversation by saying 'I am sorry that things are difficult for you. If you would like, we can make an arrangement to speak more privately.'

● Practicalities

Getting to know your students

The number of personal tutees assigned to each tutor varies from institution to institution but is usually around 24. The model of personal tutoring which operates in your institution will partly define how regularly you are likely to see those students. I have some students who never come to see me and only contact me when they need a reference. There are others who I see at least weekly.

Your job will be easier if you know your students. Investing time at the beginning of their course will reap rich rewards in the future. This can be managed by making arrangements to see all the tutees as a distinct group, which has the benefit to the tutor of saving a considerable amount of time at a very busy time of the year. This will increase the students' opportunities to make friends in the early days when they may feel isolated and homesick. In my first year I did not maximise the opportunity that early meetings with my tutees could have afforded. I assumed that students had already formed the beginnings of a relationship with others.

Today's modular courses mean that students do not necessarily live and work alongside the same students, making it easy for them to become withdrawn and isolated, and so the personal tutor can be someone who is interested in who they are, where they are from and what they were doing before university. This will help raise their esteem and confidence. Being part of a tutorial group can help the transition from living as part of a close family to communal living and can be one of the few constants in their undergraduate years.

Practical suggestions

- ☐ Ensure that you have sent a group email message at the very beginning of the year so that a welcome from you is waiting when they first access their university email.

- ☐ Hold a coffee morning and invite them all along to meet you and each other.

- ☐ Use ice breakers to help them get to know you and each other. Laughter can be particularly powerful at this time. There are a number of easily accessible resources on the internet, such as www.funandgames.org.

- ☐ Encourage them to use their university email addresses rather than personal ones as they may contain some sexual connotation and are therefore rejected by the university server as junk mail.

- ☐ Encourage them to swap email addresses and mobile phone numbers so that they can operate as a mutual support system.

- ☐ To facilitate the development of the relationship receive as much information about students as they would like to give. This also reinforces your interest in them as individuals.

- ☐ Encourage tutees to participate in a discussion board in your institution's virtual environment.

Transition from home to university

The personal tutor can assist with this process by raising the topic of homesickness at the first group tutorial, which will enable students to see it as a normal part of the process of beginning university, and offer them the opportunity to support each other.

Jenny, an eighteen-year-old student, seemingly floundered from the very beginning of her course. When I first met her at the initial group tutorial I was aware that she seemed to lack the social skills to introduce herself to others and to form new relationships. At the time I put this down to nervousness. After the first tutorial she didn't come to see me and I didn't chase her, assuming that 'no news is good news'. When I heard that she had left the course mid-way through the first semester I telephoned her and she told me that she had felt alone and frightened from the very beginning. I pressed her to try and tell me what I could have done that might have made a difference. She felt that if there had been a requirement to come and see me on her own after the first group meeting, she would have done so and perhaps told me that she was struggling. However, she couldn't conceive of anything that I could have done that would have kept her on the course. It became apparent as we spoke that, as I had expected, the issue was not about the course, it was about her transition between home and university.

In such circumstances it seems as if the student's ability to successfully navigate this transition is about making the strange, familiar. One of the difficulties with this is that this process happens with time, which means that the student has to survive the intervening months while the change is gradually integrated into their life. A number of strategies may help their short-term coping:

- Accepting that others also feel as they do.
- Maintaining an appropriate amount of contact with home. Too much can mean that they never feel settled in one place. Too little may result in feeling disconnected from sources of support at home such as family and friends.
- Keeping busy by joining the activities of a variety of clubs and societies can fill the initial long days away from home.

Making appointments

This is largely a matter of personal preference. Many institutions prefer staff to put a timetable on their doors so that students can see availability; however, this can be a problem for part-time students or those on split campuses. It also means that tutorial commitments are made a long time ahead, which can reduce flexibility. Appointments made weeks in advance in this way can be problematic for staff as they often find that a number of students sign up but don't turn up.

Insights

In one week I had six students who failed to turn up for pre-booked appointments. It makes me less willing to put myself out. It is such a waste of time and often I have had to turn away other students, whose need might have been greater, because I was fully booked. The biggest problem is when they book using the timetable on the door. For some reason they think it's alright to change their mind and just not turn up rather than letting me know. It's also very rare for them to apologise afterwards for not attending. I do get better attendance from those who book by email or phone.

Electronic communication

Where much of the support that you provide to students is provided online it is important to focus on the impact of the written word. Emails, which are often brief and written in an abbreviated form, may be interpreted as harsh or cold.

Practical suggestions

- ☐ Use emoticons to soften the communication by conveying feelings.

- ☐ Begin and end with a cheery greeting.

- ☐ If you don't have time to reply fully to an email do send back a very brief (if necessary, automated) response to reassure the student that you have received their message and that you will get back to them.

- ☐ Avoid writing in capital letters in emails – it is the electronic equivalent of shouting.

- ☐ Keep a copy of all emails that you send to students.

- ☐ Set up an email receipt system so that you have a record of your contact.

- ☐ Ensure that your emails end with a relatively informal automatic signature rather than your name and position.

Managing the tutorial

Lago and Shipton (1994) suggest that there are three main reasons why a student will contact their personal tutor. They come because they have been sent for, because they need support/guidance, and to celebrate. It is important to clarify at the beginning of the tutorial why the student has come. The motivation for the visit will define the approach that the tutor takes, which can save time and misunderstandings. When I first meet my tutees I explain to them that it will help me to help them if when they email for a tutorial they put the reason in the subject box. This enables me to gather any necessary information before I see the student. The word 'personal' in the heading alerts me that the tutorial may take more time than I would otherwise have allowed. Otherwise you might try 'How can I help?' or 'What would you like to talk about today?' The use of open questions is likely to illicit a more considered and therefore helpful response. The use of closed questions will limit the response and leave you guiding the tutorial.

Time constraints

Being clear about time boundaries will help you stay in control of your day. Tell the student at the beginning how much time you have – 'We have ten minutes today.' Then make another appointment rather than overrun. You might say 'this is obviously important and needs more time', then arrange another meeting. The same technique can be used to manage students who stop you in the corridor or who drop in at your office when you do not have the time to see them. In common with counselling clients some students will wait until they are just going out of the door to say that which is most important to them. It is perfectly acceptable to respond by saying something like 'This sounds very important to you, let's make an appointment and put aside some time to discuss it.' If you are hoping to keep to your timetable for tutorials it is important not to interrupt them to answer the phone or the door. To do so may give the student the message that they do not have your full attention, and inevitably the tutorial overruns as you try to make up the time you spent on the interruptions.

Boundaries

It is important to consider in advance of meeting with students how much you are willing to involve yourself in their personal matters. This will vary from tutor to tutor. Some personal tutors will be very clear in their boundaries and wish to remain uninvolved, not wishing to listen to or become involved in students' personal issues. This will mean that they need to refer students on at the very earliest opportunity. Others will be prepared to spend time listening to students before deciding whether other sources of help are appropriate.

The boundaries which you put in place will also depend upon the kind of relationship that you have with your students. I have colleagues who give their mobile telephone number to their personal tutees and who are willing to accept both texts and calls. For some this obviously makes access to the tutor easier, which may mean that they can address small issues before they become large ones. Personally, I feel that this crosses a line, intruding into my personal life, and is therefore not an action that I would take.

Record-keeping

There may be occasions when you will be asked for a record of your meetings. This is particularly likely where the students' PDP are part of the tutorial process. This record will also prove invaluable if the student uses the appeals procedure, claims mitigating circumstances, or when you need to write a reference for them.

The students have a right under data protection legislation to see everything that is written about them. When keeping records of personal tutorials it is therefore advisable to record only the facts, avoiding feelings and attitudes. If you have recorded information about a student you also have a responsibility to keep it secure. You can minimise risk by adopting a numbering system for students and ensuring that the key to the system is not kept in the office with your records. Students are entitled to know:

- What information is held about them and why.
- How to access the information and have it corrected, erased, and kept up to date.

Confidentiality

Counsellors are bound by a professional code of ethics which prohibits them from discussing what a student has told them unless they believe the safety of the student or another is at risk. Other university staff are unlikely to be bound by the same restrictions but they should still consider how they will treat what students tell them. I usually explain to my students that they can talk to me in confidence but if I feel that I can best help them by talking to someone else then I will discuss it with them first. There are some exceptions to the confidentiality that you can offer students. These include:

- Having knowledge of a crime.
- Abuse that involves a child.

I had developed a good relationship with Tracy throughout her course. During her second semester she telephoned me and asked to see me urgently. She seemed very upset and I arranged to see her the same day. She appeared shocked and struggled to tell me what had happened at home. Tracy had found out the day before that her nephew (a 14-year-old boy) had sexually abused her six-year-old daughter. She told me that she had told no one and that she did not know what to do. As I am an early childhood lecturer she hoped that I would help her to decide what to do. I knew that the abuse needed to be reported. As we talked I was able to encourage her to make the contact with social services herself. With my support she telephoned social services and so was able to begin the process of addressing the needs of both victim and abuser

Although this kind of intervention will, hopefully, be very rare, this case study highlights the part that we might be called upon to play in very complex situations. When there is a need to involve a third party it is always more appropriate to encourage the student to involve others themselves rather than have you do it on their behalf.

Disability discrimination
The key to supporting students and facilitating compliance with the Disability Discrimination Act (2001) is to follow the Code of Practice in creating a culture and atmosphere which is open and welcoming, so that students feel safe enough to disclose disability. In this way reasonable adjustments can be made to support their learning.

Bharti, a first-year student, who I had got to know reasonably well, told me that she had experienced some acute bouts of anxiety since her early teens, for which she was receiving treatment. She had not disclosed this on entry and so the university was unaware of her possible support needs. She was reluctant to make it known since she viewed university as a fresh start and feared that she would be judged as weak. I was able to encourage her to discuss her needs with a student support adviser, who was able to put in place a discreet support package which I think enabled her to manage the impact of her anxiety on her work. Without this I think she would have struggled to remain on the course. I hope that the non-judgemental response that I tried to demonstrate helped her to accept that this might be true of others and enabled her to accept the support that was available to her.

I have often received telephone calls from parents, other family members or friends who are worried about a student. This creates a difficult situation since most students are over 18 and classified as adults. University policy is usually not to discuss a student without their permission. This can be difficult when you are approached by a concerned parent. I usually listen to the concerns and then offer to contact the student and let them know that contact has been made.

When you are concerned for a student's well being

Being the sole confidante of a student in distress is extremely time consuming and personally debilitating. It is therefore important to recognise that you might not be the best person to offer the support that they need. Most institutions' Student Services departments circulate recommendations for how to respond to students for whom you are concerned. The key is to establish an early relationship with the student so that they will feel comfortable seeking and accepting help if things begin to go wrong.

Practical suggestions

☐ It is important to remember that you are not responsible for solving a student's problems.

☐ Try not to give advice. This is usually based on your experiences and so may be inappropriate. It also reduces the chances of the student taking responsibility for their own life.

☐ Take the opportunity to discuss the student, without giving recognisable details, with the university counsellor or Student Services adviser.

☐ If you remain concerned, ask the student for permission to contact their GP.

Personal safety

Paramount in the work that we do should be our own safety. As most institutions now work a 9 a.m. to 9 p.m. day it is possible to find yourself seeing a student in a deserted area of the campus. Arrange your office so that your seat is between the student and the door. This will leave you with a clear exit route. If you leave your seat to open the office door, put a book on it – the student will usually take the empty chair.

A number of male colleagues have discussed their disquiet at meeting female students in their offices. This is usually addressed by ensuring meetings take place in public areas. In the summer some are to be found sitting on seats outside in the grounds, at other times a corner of the canteen serves as an impromptu office. Care needs to be taken with the message that this could send to students about the informal nature of the relationship.

Immediate student support needs

The story of the student in Chapter 4 who just wanted to tell her tutor 'that my Mum died' raises awareness that as personal tutors we are not organised as an emergency service. It is hard to recognise and accept that sometimes there may be no one available to connect with students in distress in a timely manner. However, the reality of everyday working life is that staff do have other working commitments and responsibilities. It does highlight the importance of ensuring that there is a system of fast-tracking support in some circumstances. Most universities will have a Student Services reception which students can approach for immediate help, but these are rarely, if ever, available 24 hours a day. Consequently, it is important for institutions to recognise that all staff who come into contact with students need to have an understanding of how they can refer students to specialist help in an emergency. Students may approach an administrator or other member of support staff as these will be around when academic staff are teaching or caught up in meetings. This is best achieved through a robust training programme for all staff rather than just academic staff.

Support for the personal tutor

The nature of the personal tutoring role is that academic staff are often isolated and there is therefore potential for them to be overwhelmed by the concerns of their students. Ridley (2006) asks 'Who is looking after me?' – highlighting the concern of lecturers, particularly those new to the profession, that there is the potential to be overwhelmed by the diverse needs of so many students. Lecturers do not receive the 'over-seeing' (Nelson Jones, 2005) or supervision required of their counsellor colleagues, yet hear many of the same issues. The aim of this supervision is to provide regular opportunities for consultation and support with another practitioner. This enables the counsellor to reflect on the interventions that they have made. Personal tutors need to rely on making similar opportunities to discuss difficult stories with a trusted colleague. There is no need to reveal the student's personal details, thereby respecting any confidentiality promises that you may have made to the student.

As a personal tutor it is possible to spend a great deal of time with a particular student and become entrenched in their problems. As a result we begin to see the smaller rather than the bigger picture. Discussion with colleagues can enable a refocusing to the bigger screen. Ridley (2006) emphasises the value that tutors place on this collegiate response but this needs to be available to all tutors and incorporated into a framework recognised by institutions as an integral part of the student support systems.

The seemingly limitless nature of the relationship between tutor and tutee can add to existing stresses which Edworthy (2002) identifies as being prevalent in higher education: workloads, communication, changes, interpersonal relationships, and insufficient support/lack of resources. These stresses are compounded where there is role ambiguity, which occurs when a worker is expected to perform his or her duties without receiving adequate details about the scope and responsibilities of the job (Edworthy, 2002). Personal tutoring would seem to come into this category.

Therefore the ability to recognise your own limitations is important for both your own well being and that of the student. Usually Heads of Student Services or Counselling Services will make themselves available to personal tutors to discuss difficult situations and offer support. Tutors who feel that they need further support should make their need known to the Personnel Department as the institution does have a joint responsibility with staff for their health and well being. Universities, in common with other employers, have a 'duty of care' under the Health and Safety at Work Act 1974 to ensure people are not made ill by their work. The Health and Safety Executive (HSE) (2004) introduced Management Standards aimed at helping employers assess the risks arising from hazards at work, including work-related stress. These require that employers assess risk to staff health and take reasonable steps to prevent harm.

● **Key skills**

There are a number of key skills that will help facilitate a positive relationship with your students:

Empathy
Empathy is the ability to make another person feel understood. This can be achieved using a combination of the skills presented here, but the core skill is to focus on what the student is feeling. For example, a student who is anxious, upset or nervous may need time to relax sufficiently to tell you what is on their mind. If they appear to be struggling to know what to say, try

describing what you see – for example, 'You look sad/anxious etc.' This will help them to feel understood before they have even said anything.

Being non-judgemental

Students will only feel free to discuss issues that may be troubling them if they feel that they are not being judged. It means not imposing your own values and belief systems on them, and so you are accepting of them as individuals. It helps to remember that most of us are doing the best that we can to manage our lives.

Listening

The skill of listening is likely to be the most important that you can use in your relationship with your personal tutee. This needs to begin with demonstrating to the student that you are listening and that they are being heard.

Practical suggestions

☐ Ensure that there are opportunities for you to listen without interruptions.

☐ Use non-verbal behaviour to demonstrate your interest in what is being said, e.g. nodding, eye contact.

☐ Don't underestimate the power of giving a student your time. Listening to their story may enable some to move forward from a difficult period.

Reena's story is an example of the value of effective listening.

Reena told me that she couldn't 'thank her tutor enough', highlighting the value of effective personal tutoring. As we talked she realised that she hadn't thanked her at all and so expressed concern that her personal tutor might not know how much her help had mattered. She had found it difficult to express her gratitude, and I wondered whether she herself did not understand its value at the time. There seemed to be an element of embarrassment at what she perceived as her past need, and she didn't feel able to bring up the past with the tutor. We looked together at ways that she might address those concerns and acknowledged the potential benefits to both her and the personal tutor in bringing about an end to the episode. She felt that too much time had elapsed to make a written or personal approach. Having discussed a number of options I made a commitment to undertake two actions on her behalf after she ➡

completed the course and left the university. First, to ensure that her personal tutor received a copy of the research and secondly, that I would follow that up by sharing what I had understood of the positive impact, for the student, of her tutor's interventions – 'She made me feel that I mattered. I can't thank her enough.' When I approached the tutor concerned, as I had promised, she was overwhelmed by the student's perception of the contribution she had made, feeling that all she had done was give the student time.

Referral

Referral is about recognising that we might not always be the person best placed to help. It is about determining what or who might be the most appropriate source of that help.

Rebecca had struggled with most of her assignments and at the end of the first semester came to talk to me about her difficulties. I asked her to return with her assignments and we went through the comments of module tutors. All of them highlighted to me the likelihood that Rebecca was dyslexic. I was aware that she needed to discuss her concerns with staff in the Equal Opportunities Centre in order that she might undergo testing and receive the appropriate support to enable her to maximise her learning and I therefore wanted to refer her appropriately. She was very reluctant, feeling that there was some shame attached to asking for help. I was able to use counselling skills to encourage her to look towards the rest of her degree course and predict the outcome. This gave her the necessary motivation to approach those who could help. She returned to see me many times after her diagnosis and rather than the feelings of failure that she had anticipated she surprised herself by feeling relieved that there was a reason for the struggle that she had experienced all through her school years.

As with all student support the challenge is to recognise when it is appropriate to help the student yourself and when to refer on. At the beginning this was a very conscious process for me which I triggered by having within my line of vision information leaflets on Student Support Services and other local and national referral agencies, which I could pass on to students when appropriate. In the cases of issues such as dyslexia, most higher education institutions will have guidelines and support for staff that tutors can dip into.

The point of referral will be different for each tutor-and-student relationship and will depend on a variety of factors:

- nature of the student/tutor relationship;
- level of experience/skills of the tutor;
- time available;
- nature of the difficulty.

Referrals need to be handled sensitively as students can perceive it as rejection, and may feel vulnerable after confiding their troubles.

Chapters 3 and 4 highlight the range of issues that students might bring to the tutorial. In order to respond to these, tutors will find it helpful to have an awareness of support agencies. A range of these is presented here, but most Student Services departments will make available, through their web pages, details of national and local, voluntary and statutory support agencies.

Specialist support agencies

Alcohol

Drinkline is the National Alcohol Helpline, which is a confidential alcohol counselling and information service offering the following services:

- information and self-help materials;
- help to callers worried about their own drinking;
- support for the family and friends of people who are drinking;
- advice to callers on where to go for help.

Telephone (Helpline): 0800 917 8282

Alcohol Concern is the national agency on alcohol misuse. They work to reduce the incidence and costs of alcohol-related harm and to increase the range and quality of services available to people with alcohol-related problems.

Drugs
National Drugs Helpline
Website: www.release.org.uk
Telephone (Heroin Helpline): 0845 4500 215

Mental Health
SANE is one of the UK's leading charities concerned with improving the lives of everyone affected by mental illness.
Website: http://sane.org.uk
Telephone (Helpline): 0845 767 8000

Samaritans
Website: www.samaritans.org.uk
Telephone (Helpline): 08457 90 90 90

Relationships
Relate offers advice, relationship counselling, sex therapy, workshops, mediation, consultations and support face-to-face, by phone and through their website: http://relate.org.uk

Self harm
Young People and Self Harm is a key information resource for young people who self harm, their friends and families, and professionals working with them.
Website: http://selfharm.org.uk

Stress
Stress Busting
Website: http://stressbusting.co.uk

● Continuing professional development

Postgraduate Certificate in Teaching in Higher Education
This qualification is now usually mandatory for all permanent academic staff teaching more than 0.5 full-time equivalent who have less than five years' experience of teaching in higher education. These courses lead to a certificate from both individual institutions and the national body of SEDA (the Staff and Educational Development Association). Most courses are also recognised by the Higher Education Academy and may lead to professional accreditation. The objectives require that by the end of the course candidates will have:

- Designed a teaching programme
- Used a wide and appropriate range of teaching and learning methods
- Provided support to students on academic and pastoral matters
- Used a wide range of assessment techniques
- Used a range of monitoring and evaluation techniques
- Performed teaching support and academic administrative tasks
- Developed personal and professional coping strategies
- Gained an appreciation of the pedagogic concerns of [their] subject discipline

- Reflected on [their] own personal and professional practice and development.

These objectives are informed and underpinned by the following values:

- Understanding of how students learn
- Concern for student development
- Commitment to scholarship
- Team working
- Practising equal opportunities
- Continued reflection on professional practice
- Scholarship and disciplinary inquiry
- Personal values and goals

(SEDA, 2005, p. 1)

This qualification requires that students demonstrate their achievement of the objectives; this is usually but not exclusively provided through the compilation of a portfolio of evidence. To demonstrate an ability to provide support to students on academic and pastoral matters it is useful to keep a reflective journal of interactions with students. This can then be used to support your assertions. This book will also provide suggestions on ways in which you might provide the appropriate support.

I began my Postgraduate Certificate as soon as I took up the post, as required by my institution; however, I now feel it would be more appropriate for new staff to settle into their roles and develop an understanding of systems and procedures before beginning the course. In the early days it was difficult to work out what evidence would be relevant and appropriate and although I was committed to ensuring that quality exceeded quantity there were areas where I adopted a 'supermarket trolley approach' (Brown, 2000, p. 98). This was generated by a fear of not producing sufficient evidence to fulfil the criteria. The portfolio can become a weighty burden as it is undertaken at a time when the tutor is new to the role, and perhaps struggling with new responsibilities. Cox (1996) suggests that its compilation does serve to remind the practitioner of the difficulty and significance of the work that we do.

As the aim of this book is not to revisit the work undertaken by others, but to bring together suggestions for best practice, a deeper understanding of the pastoral role can be achieved with the relevant further reading suggested at the end of this chapter.

Other training

Many staff in higher education will already have professional registration within an education or health and social care setting and therefore have undertaken training and or qualifications in counselling skills. These skills are not necessary for the work, as the key skill is the ability to be empathic, but tutors may find it easier to respond to the needs of their tutees within the skills framework that a short course would provide. These courses are often offered as a regular part of the staff development programme.

There are a number of useful texts for personal tutors who would like to develop their helping skills further. Those listed here are a starting point:

Geldard, K. and Geldard, D. (2005), *Practical Counselling Skills: An Integrative Approach* (Basingstoke: Palgrave Macmillan).

Geldard, K. and Geldard, D. (2003), *Counselling Skills in Everyday Life* (Basingstoke: Palgrave Macmillan).

Nelson Jones, R. (2005), *Practical Counselling and Helping Skills* (London: Sage).

Thompson, N. (2006), *People Problems* (Basingstoke: Palgrave Macmillan).

Practical suggestions

☐ Clarify at the very beginning of the tutorial why the student has come. It can save misunderstandings and time.

☐ Being clear about time boundaries will help you stay in control of your day.

☐ Keep a record of every meeting with each personal tutee.

☐ Investing time at the beginning of a course will reap rich rewards in the future.

☐ Develop a knowledge of local and national support agencies to whom you can refer students when their needs fall outside your capabilities.

☐ Develop a mutual support relationship with a trusted colleague.

☐ Make sure that your employer is aware of any impact of the work on your well being.

● **Further reading**

Bassman, S. (1984), 'Students' Perceptions of Personal Problems, Appropriate Help Sources, and General Attitudes about Counselling', *Journal of College Student Personnel*, 25, pp. 139–45.

Easton, E. and Van Laar, D. (1995) 'Experiences of Lecturers Helping Distressed Students in Higher Education', *British Journal of Guidance and Counselling*, 23: 2, pp. 173–8.

Heads of University Counselling Services (1999), *The Impact of Increasing Levels of Psychological Disturbance amongst Students in Higher Education*, www.rhbnc.ac.uk/~uhye099/hucsreport.html (accessed 9 February 2004).

Higher Education Quality Unit (1996), *Personal Tutoring and Academic Advice in Focus* (London: Higher Education Quality Council).

Hixenbaugh, P., Thomas, L. and Barfield, S. (eds) (2006), *Personal Tutoring in Higher Education* (Stoke on trent: Trentham).

Lago, C. and Shipton, G. (1994), *Personal Tutoring in Action* (Sheffield: University Counselling Service, Sheffield University).

Lomax, C. (2004), 'Helping University Staff to Help Students', *Association of University and College Counsellors*, Summer 2004: 5–8.

Mental Health Foundation (MHF) (2001), *Promoting Student Mental Health* (MHF) www.mentalhealth.org.uk/publications/?entryId (accessed 7 May 2005).

Roberts, R. (2002), *Student Living Report: The Definitive Study of the Student Experience* www.mori.com/polls/2001/unite.shtml (accessed 9 January 2006).

Royal College of Psychiatrists (2003), *The Mental Health of Students in Higher Education*, London Council Report CR112.

Stanley, N. and Manthorpe, J. (eds) (2002), *Students' Mental Health Needs: Problems and Responses* (London: Jessica Kingsley).

University of Leicester (2002), *Student Psychological Health Project* http://le.ac.uk/edsc/sphp (accessed 12 May 2004).

Reflections

Lindsey Neville

This book has emphasised the importance of the role of the personal tutor in students' learning. It has not sought to provide all the answers but to highlight the complexity of the work and to begin an exploration of the areas which need developing. Practical suggestions have been made for delivering personal tutoring by providing effective support for all. It does prescribe a system of personal tutoring as the needs of different courses and institutions will vary. The suggested model of good practice is applicable to many different personal tutoring systems. It has concentrated on supporting personal tutors with the practical aspects of the work. It leaves a number of questions which may need additional consideration by individuals and institutions, together with areas which would benefit from further research.

- Should there be a common model of personal tutoring?
- Should personal tutoring be delivered only by those with a greater aptitude or an interest in the work?
- Do individual personal tutors have sufficient/appropriate training and support to undertake the role?
- What are the boundaries of the role?
- How can employers provide protected, dedicated time for the role?
- How should students be allocated to personal tutors?
- What is the responsibility of the student in this relationship?
- How can privacy issues be addressed?
- How can staff safety be ensured?
- Should there be a minimum requirement for students to attend tutorials and should they be penalised in any way if they fail to attend?
- Where and how should records of tutorials be maintained?
- How can universities enhance the role of personal tutoring?
- What emphasis should be placed on PDP in this relationship?
- What role can administrative staff play in student support?
- What is the impact of positive personal tutoring on academic outcome?
- Should personal tutor meetings be allocated in the timetable?

References

Association of University Administrators (AUA), Higher Education Equal Opportunities Network (HEEON) and Equality Challenge Unit (ECU) (March 2005), *A–Z of Equality and Diversity* (London: AUA, HEEON and ECU).

Association of University College Counsellors (1999), *A Report from the Heads of University Counselling Services – Degrees of Disturbance: The New Agenda* (Rugby: BACP).

Association of University College Counsellors (2005), *Annual Survey of Counselling in Further and Higher Education, 2003/04* (Rugby: BACP).

Bell, E. (1996), *Counselling in Higher Education* (Buckingham: Open University Press).

Bell, E. (1997), 'Counselling in Higher Education', in S. Palmer and G. McMahon (eds), *Handbook of Counselling*, 2nd edn (London: Tavistock/Routledge).

Berne, E. (1964), *Games People Play*, 4th edn (New York: Ballantine).

Bolton, G. (1999), *The Therapeutic Potential of Creative Writing Myself* (London: Jessica Kingsley).

British Association for Counseling and Psychology (BACP) (2005), *Ethical Framework*, www.bacp.co.uk/ethical_framework/ (accessed 20 March 2005).

British Association for Counseling and Psychology (BACP) (2006), *What is Counselling?* www.bacp.co.uk/education/whatiscounselling.html (accessed 27 November 2006).

Brown, S. (2000) 'Assessing Practice', in S. Brown and A. Glasner (eds), *Assessment Matters in Higher Education*, 2nd edn (Bury St Edmunds: Society for Research into Education).

Camelot Foundation and Mental Health Foundation (2006), *The Truth about Self Harm*, www.mentalhealth.org.uk/publications/?EntryID=45371 (accessed 28 November 2006).

Carroll, M. and Walton, M. (1997), *A Handbook of Counselling in Organisations* (London: Sage).

Centre for Instructional Development and Research (CIDR), University of Washington (online) (2006), available from: www.depts.washington.edu/cidrweb/inclusive/background.html (accessed on 7 November 2006).

Centre for Media, Arts and Performance, Coventry School of Art and Design, Coventry University (2006), *Same but Different: Working Effectively with Student Diversity* (DVD Training Resource pack), Coventry University.

Centre for Teaching and Learning (CTL), University of Minnesota (online) (2006), *Cultural/Ethnic Disparity in Advising*, available from: www.umn.edu/ohr/teachlearn/resouces/diversity/advising.html (accessed 7 November 2006).

Church of England Report by the Board of Education (2005), *Aiming Higher: Higher Education and the Church's Mission* (London: General Synod of the Church of England).

Clough, Peter (2002), *Narratives and Fictions in Educational Research* (Buckingham: Open University).

Corey, G. (1991), *Theory and Practice of Counselling and Psychotherapy*, 4th edn (Belmont, Calif.: Wadsworth).

Cottrell, S. (2003), *Study Skills Handbook* (Basingstoke: Palgrave Macmillan).

Cox, P. (1996), 'Becoming a Portfolio Person – Learning to Learn', http://www.peterdcox.me.uk.pcox.nsf/dx/21072004185006PDCNWV.htm, accessed 12 May 2007.

Dearing, R. (1997), *Summary Report: The National Committee of Inquiry into Higher Education* (Norwich: HMSO).

Department for Education and Skills (online), 17 November 2006, *Guidance for Higher Education Providers to Help Tackle Violent Extremism in the Name of Islam on Campus*, available from: www.dfes.gov.uk/pns/pnaattach/20060170/1.txt (accessed 18 November 2006).

Department of Health (1998), *Our Healthier Nation* (London: HMSO).

Dryden, W. (1991), *A Dialogue with Arnold Lazarus: 'It Depends'* (Milton Keynes: Open University Press).

Earwaker, J. (1992), *Helping and Supporting Students: Re-thinking the Issues* (Buckingham: Buckingham Society for Research into Higher Education, and Open University).

Easton, E. and Van Laar, D. (1995), 'Experiences of Lecturers Helping Distressed Students in Higher Education', *British Journal of Guidance and Counselling*, 23: 2, 173–8.

Edworthy, A. (ed.) (2002), *Managing Stress – Managing Universities and Colleges: Guides to Good Practice* (Buckingham: Open University Press).

Egan, G. (1990), *Skilled Helper*, 4th edn (London: Wadsworth).

Equality Challenge Unit (ECU) (November 2004), *Equality is Challenging . . . Positive Action* (London: Equality Challenge Unit).

Equality Challenge Unit (August 2005), *Equal Opportunities: An Introduction* (London: Equality Challenge Unit).

Freudenberger, H. J. (1980), *Burnout: The High Cost of High Achievement* (London: Arrow).

Gabbard, G. and Topeka, K. (2000), 'Disguise or Consent: Problems and Recommendations concerning the Publication and Presentation of Clinical Material', *International Journal of Psychoanalysis*, 81, p. 107.

Geldard, K. and Geldard, D. (2003), *Counselling Skills in Everyday Life* (Basingstoke: Palgrave Macmillan).

Gidman, J. (2001), 'The Role of the Personal Tutor: a Literature Review', *Nurse Education Today*, 21, pp. 359–65.

Gilbert, S. (1989), 'The Juggling Act of the College Counselling Center', *The Counselling Psychologist*, 17: 3, pp. 477–89.

Grant, A. (2002), 'Identifying Students' Concerns: Taking a Whole Institutional Approach', in N. Stanley and J. Manthorpe (eds), *Student Mental Health Needs: Problems and Responses* (London: Jessica Kingsley).

Grant, A, (2004), 'Alcohol and Student Success', *Association for University and College Counselling Journal*, Winter, 18–21.

Grant, A, (2006), 'Personal Tutoring: a System in Crisis', in L. Thomas and P. Hixenbaugh (eds), *Personal Tutoring in Higher Education* (Stoke on Trent: Trentham Books).

Grant, A. (in press), 'Student Services in the United Kingdom – an Overview', in K. J. Osfield and Associates (eds), *The Internationalization of Student Affairs and Services in Higher Education: An Emerging Global Perspective* (Washington: NASPA).

Hart, N. (1996), 'The Role of the Tutor in a College of Further Education: a Comparison of Skills used by Personal Tutors and by Student Counsellors when Working with Students in Distress', *British Journal of Guidance and Counselling*, 24: 83–96.

Heads of University Counselling Services (1999), *The Impact of Increasing Levels of Psychological Disturbance amongst Students in Higher Education*, www.rhbnc.ac.uk/~uhye099/hucsreport.html (accessed 9 February 2004).

Heads of University Counselling Services (HUCS) (2002), *Survey of Medical, Psychiatric and Counselling Provision in Higher Education*, www.hucs.org.uk (accessed 9 January 2005).

Heads of University Counselling Services (HUCS) (2003), 'Beyond the Individual: Roles Offered by University Counselling Services', www.hucs.org/caleb.htm (accessed 8 May 2007).

Health and Safety Executive (2004), *Working Together to Reduce Stress at Work: A Guide for Employees*, www.hse.gov.uk/pubns/misc686.pdf (accessed 25 October 2006.

Hewitt, E. and Wheeler, S. (2004), 'Counselling in Higher Education: the Experience of the Lone Counsellor', *British Journal of Guidance and Counselling*, 32:4, pp. 533–45.

Higher Education Quality Unit (1996), *Personal Tutoring and Academic Advice in Focus* (London: Higher Education Quality Council).

Higher Education Statistics Agency (2005), *Statistics online*, www.hesa.ac.uk/holisdocs/pubinfo/stud.htm (accessed 19 February 2007).

Higher Education Statistics Agency (2006), *Performance Indicators in Higher*

Education in the UK 2004/05, www.hesa.ac.uk/pi/0405/continuation.htm (accessed 6 November 2006)

Hodges, C. and Smith, T. (2002), *The Student Living Report* (London: Mori).

Hughes, R, and Hardey, J. (2002), *Feeling at Home*, 3rd edn (London: The British Council).

Inter Faith Network for the United Kingdom (2005), *Building Good Relations with People of Different Faiths and Beliefs* (London: Inter Faith Network for the UK).

Jackson, S., Ajayi, S. and Quigley, M. (2005), *Going to University from Care* (London: Institute of Education, University of London and The Frank Buttle Trust).

Jaques, D. (1989), *Personal Tutoring* (Oxford: Oxford Centre for Staff Development).

Johnston, V. (2000), *Identifying Students at Risk of Non-Progression: The Development of a Diagnostic Test* (Cardiff: BERA).

Lago, C. and Shipton, G. (1994), *Personal Tutoring in Action* (Sheffield: University Counselling Service).

Lees, J. and Vaspe, A. (1999), *Clinical Counselling in Further and Higher Education* (London: Routledge).

Lomax, C. (2004), 'Helping University Staff to Help Students', *Association of University and College Counsellors Journal*, Summer 2004: 5–8.

Maslach, C. and Jackson, S. E. (1981), 'The Measurement of Experienced Burnout', *Journal of Occupational Behaviour*, 5 (9), pp. 176–82.

May, R. (1999), 'Doing Clinical Work in a College or University', in J. Lees and A. Vaspe, *Clinical Counselling in Further and Higher Education* (London: Routledge).

McGivney, V, (1996), 'Staying or Leaving the Course: Non-Completion and Retention of Mature Students in Further and Higher Education' (Leicester: NIACE).

McLeod, J. (1999), 'Counselling as a Social Process', *Counselling*, 10: 3, pp. 217–22.

McNair, S. (1997), *Getting the Most out of HE: Supporting Learner Autonomy* (Sheffield: Department for Employment and Education).

Mental Health Foundation (2001), *Promoting Student Mental Health*, www.mentalhealth.org.uk/html/content (accessed 2 March 2004).

National Audit Office (2002) *Improving Student Achievement in English Higher Education* (London: The Stationery Office).

National Union of Students and Trade Union Congress (2006), *All Work and Low Pay: The Growth in UK Student Employment*, www.tuc.org.uk/extras/allworklowpay.pdf (accessed 15 October 2006).

Nelson-Jones, R. (2001), *Theory and Practice of Counselling and Therapy* (London: Sage).

Nelson-Jones, R. (2005), *Practical Counselling and Helping Skills* (London: Sage).

Neville, L. (2004), 'Counselling in Further Education', in M. Reid (ed.), *Counselling in Different Settings* (Basingstoke: Palgrave Macmillan).

Noonan, E. (1983), *Counselling Young People* (London: Methuen).

O'Mahoney, P. and O'Brien, S. (1980), 'Demographic and Social Characteristics of University Students Attending a Psychiatrist', *British Journal of Psychiatry*, 137, pp. 547–50.

Orbach, S. (2001), 'Is there a Place for Emotional Literacy in the Learning Environment?', *Counselling and Psychotherapy Journal*, vol. 12, no. 3 (April 2001), pp. 4–7.

Owen, M. (2002), '"Sometimes You Feel you're in Niche Time": the Personal Tutor System, a Case Study', *Active Learning in Higher Education,* vol. 3, no. 1, pp. 7–23.

Palmer, S. and McMahon, G. (eds) (1997), *Handbook of Counselling*, 2nd edn (London: Tavistock/Routledge).

Patel, U. (2003), 'Real World Learning', *Higher Education Review*, 36: 1, pp. 89–91.

Persaud, R. (2001), *Staying Sane: How to Make Your Mind Work* (London: Bantam).

Prosser, M. and Trigwell, K. (2001), *Understanding Learning and Teaching: The Experience in Higher Education* (Buckingham: Open University Press).

QAA (2001), *Guidelines for HE Progress Files*, www.qaa.ac.uk/academic infrastructure/progressFiles/guidelines/progfile2001.asp (accessed 15 October 2006).

QAA (2004), *Code of Practice for the Assurance of Academic Quality and Standards in Higher Education* www.qaa.ac.uk/academicinfrastructure/ codeofpractice/section2/default.asp (accessed 20 October 2005).

Race, P. (2001), *2000 Tips for Trainers and Staff Developers* (London: Routledge).

Rana, R. (2000), *Counselling Students: A Psychodynamic Perspective* (London: Macmillan Press).

Ratigan, B. (1989) 'Counselling in Higher Education', in W. Dryden (ed.), *Handbook of Counselling in Britian* (London: Routledge).

Rhodes, S. and Jinks, A. (2005), 'Personal Tutors' Views of their Role with Pre-registration Nursing Students: an Exploratory Study', *Nurse Education Today*, 25: 390–7.

Rickinson, B. and Rutherford, D. (1995), 'Increasing Student Retention Rates', *British Journal of Counselling and Guidance*, vol. 23: 2.

Rickinson, B. and Rutherford, D. (1995), 'Increasing Undergraduate Student Retention Rates', *British Journal of Counselling and Guidance*, 23: 2.

Ridley, P. (2006), 'Who's Looking After Me? – Supporting New Personal Tutors', in L. Thomas and P. Hixenbaugh, *Personal Tutoring in Higher Education* (Basingstoke: Palgrave Macmillan).

Rivis, V. (1996), *Personal Tutoring and Academic Advice in Focus* (London: Higher Education Quality Council).

Roberts, C., Watkins, L., Oakey, D. and Fox, R. (2003), *Education in a Changing Environment*, www.edu.salford.ac.uk/her/proceedings/papers/cr_03.rtf (accessed 6 November 2006).

Roberts, R. (2002), *Student Living Report: The Definitive Study of the Student Experience*, www.mori.com/polls/2001/unite.shtml (accessed 9 January 2005).

Roberts, R., Golding, J., Trowell, T., Reid, S. and Woodford, S. (2000), 'Mental and Physical Health in Students: the Role of Economic Circumstance', *Journal of Health Psychology*, 5: 289–97.

Rogers, C. (1967), *The Therapeutic Relationship and its Impact* (Madison: University of Wisconsin Press).

Rogers, C. (2002). *Client-Centred Therapy* (London: Constable).

Royal College of Psychiatrists (2003), *The Mental Health of Students in Higher Education* (London: Council Report CR112).

Samaritans (1998), *Suicide Statistics*, www.samaritans.org/know/information/suicide_stats.shtm (accessed 18 January 2005).

Shea, C. and Bond, T. (1997), 'Ethical Issues for the Counsellor in Organisations', in N. Stanley and J. Manthorpe (eds) (2002), *Students' Mental Health Needs: Problems and Responses* (London: Jessica Kingsley).

Staff Educational Development Association (2005), *SEDA-PDF*, www.seda.ac.uk/pdf/index.htm (accessed 10 November 2006).

Stanley, N. and Manthorpe, J. (eds) (2002), *Students' Mental Health Needs: Problems and Responses* (London: Jessica Kingsley).

Taylor, L. (2006), *University College's Union Journal*, June 2006, p. 35.

Thomas, L. (2006), 'Widening Participation and the Increased Need for Personal Tutoring', in L. Thomas and P. Hixenbaugh (eds), *Personal Tutoring in Higher Education* (Stoke on Trent: Trentham Books).

Thomas, L. and Hixenbaugh, P. (eds) (2006), *Personal Tutoring in Higher Education* (Stoke on Trent: Trentham Books).

Treacher, A. (2003), 'Ethnicity in the Academic Seminar', *Association for University and College Counselling Journal*, Winter, 20–1.

Trevithick, P. (2003), 'Overcoming Educational Disadvantage', *Association for University and College Counselling Journal*, Winter, 2–6.

Universities UK (2002a) *Management Guidelines* (London: SCOP [Standing Conference of Principals]).

Universities UK (2002b) *Student Services* (London: SCOP).

Universities UK (2002c), November 2002, *Student Services: Effective Approaches to Retaining Students in Higher Education* (London: Universities UK).

Universities UK (2006), *Part-time Students and Part-Time Study in Higher Education in the UK, Strand 3: A Survey of Students' Attitudes and Experiences of Part time Study and its Costs 2005/06* (London: Universities UK).

Universities UK (online) (17 November 2006), Media Release: 'Universities UK Response to DfES Guidance', www.universitiesuk.ac.uk/mediaareleases/show.asp?MR=473 (accessed 18 November 2006).

University College Worcester (2004), *Facts and Figures*, www.worc.ac.uk/cms/template.cfm?name=facts_and_figures (accessed 18 January 2005).

University of Lancaster (2002), *Student Mental Health Planning, Guidance and Training Manual*, www.studentmentalhealth.org.uk/ (accessed 1 November 2006).

University of Leicester (2002), *Student Psychological Health Project*, http.//le.ac.uk/edsc/sphp (accessed 12 May 2004).

University of York, Higher Education Academy and Institute for Access Studies, (July 2006), *Review of Widening Participation Research: Addressing the Barriers to Participation in Higher Education* (York: Higher Education Funding Council England).

Warburton, K. (1995), 'Student Counselling', *Psychodynamic Counselling*, 1: 3, pp. 421–35.

Wheeler, S. and Birtle, J. (1993), *A Handbook for Personal Tutors* (Buckingham: Open University Press).

Williams, E. (2003), 'Why UCW Students Leave: A Study of UMS Students who Withdrew in Semester 1, 2003' (unpublished).

Winston, R. B., Creamer, D. G., Miller, T. K. and Associates (2001), *The Professional Student Affairs Administrator: Educator, Leader and Manager* (Hove: Brunner-Routledge).

World Health Organisation (2001), *The World Health Report*, www.who.int/inf-pr-2001/en/pr2001-42.html (accessed 9 January 2005).

Index